GOD AND FREEDOM

GOD AND FREEDOM

ESSAYS IN HISTORICAL AND SYSTEMATIC THEOLOGY

Edited by
Colin E. Gunton
for the
Research Institute in Systematic Theology
King's College, London

T&T CLARK
EDINBURGH

T&T CLARK
59 GEORGE STREET
EDINBURGH EH2 2LQ
SCOTLAND

First Published 1995

ISBN 0 567 09725 0

British Library Cataloguing-in-Publication Data

A catalogue record for this book is available from the British Library

Typeset by Trinity Typesetting, Edinburgh
Printed and bound in Great Britain by Bookcraft, Avon

Contents

1. Introduction

Colin E. Gunton

I

In the Western theological tradition, especially since the time of Augustine, the question of the relation of divine action and human freedom has been the source of far more contention than in Eastern Orthodoxy. Augustine's teaching of radical human sinfulness, inherited from Adam and involving inevitable guilt, requires a correlative teaching that freedom derives only from a setting free, and therefore, apparently, can be realized only in dependence upon divine grace. The magisterial Reformers adopted a version of this theology, like Augustine teaching the bondage of the will apart from justifying and sanctifying divine action, even though they conceived the form of that divine action rather differently. But both the Catholic and Evangelical versions of the teaching are today widely controverted in theology, and for two reasons in particular. The first is that there is dissatisfaction with the way the teaching of original sin was formulated. The second is that the whole direction of modern thought is against it.

The heart of the modern matter is the doctrine of autonomy, which broadly speaking teaches that anything that is not in its entirety the undetermined act of the agent is, to the extent that it is not, a denial of the agent's integrity. The teaching appears at its greatest in the philosophy of Immanuel Kant, because it is there present in its most radical but also its most nuanced form, largely because of the fact that Kant makes every attempt to distance himself from a naive moral optimism. Again broadly, the teaching is that if I receive the impulse for my decisions and actions from anywhere else than the dictates of my own autonomous moral reason, they are thus far not truly my actions. Kant's successors were to apply rigorously the theological lessons of his teaching. As far as human freedom is concerned, God and the human are in competition. As Feuerbach held, the essence of the worship of God is the kind of self-abnegation that deprives the worshipper of autonomy, and that criticism has been reproduced, albeit in differing form, in both Marxism and modern liberal philosophies.

Theology must concede that the equation of God with unfreedom derives in part from the form that Christian teaching has often taken and from the way ecclesial institutions have often behaved. It cannot, however, without denying major strands of biblical teaching, go the whole way with secular doctrines of autonomy, or even, I believe, with that tendency in some Eastern Orthodox teaching also to make freedom an inherent quality of the human. For the Fourth Gospel, not only is sin a source of slavery ('Every one who commits sin is a slave to sin', Jn 8.34), but true freedom consists in being set free by the Son of God. For Paul, who, as mediated by both Augustine and Luther, tends to serve as the chief authority for the now despised Western teaching, there are diverse ways of expressing the source of the slavery — sin, the law, the principalities and powers — but the agent of freedom is the same. It is to Paul, too, that is owed the formulation of what D. M. Baillie earlier this century made famous as 'the paradox of grace'. His formulation was as follows:

> He (God) is the One who *gives* us what He demands of us, *provides* the obedience that He requires; so that we are constrained to acknowledge ... the paradox of grace, expressed in the confession: 'I ... yet not I, but the grace of God'. This is a paradox because the ascription of all the glory to God for anything good that is in us does not imply any destruction of our freedom as human personalities, but precisely the reverse: our actions are never more truly free and personal and human, they are never more truly our own, than when they are wrought in us by God.[1]

It was Augustine, in his famous dispute with Pelagius, who was responsible for the most uncompromising statement of the problem, though perhaps the most memorable formulation comes from the *Confessions*. 'Give me the grace to do as you command, and command me to do what you will':[2] apparently the most heteronomous formulation of all, especially in view of Augustine's apparent determinism and advocacy of 'irresistible grace'. But there is more to Augustine than meets the eye in this area of his thought, and he can be said to be the forerunner of more than the Reformers. As the focus of the West's particular form of the synthesis between Athens and Jerusalem, he was also the one who formulated the range of concepts which in different ways still vie for supremacy.

---

[1] D. M. Baillie, *God Was in Christ: An Essay in Incarnation and Atonement* (London: Faber, 1956), pp.144-5.
[2] Augustine, *Confessions* 10, 29, 40. The translation is something of an interpretation of the Latin, which, literally, reads: 'give what you command and command what you will' (Da quod iubes et iube quod vis).

On the one hand, there is, as we have seen, the strong anti-Pelagianism for which Augustine is so well-known. On the other hand, however, there is in Augustine a strain of autonomy theory, not in the modern sense according to which we are completely free to choose one thing or another — that tended to be God's prerogative according to Augustine, and it has only been claimed for man by modernity — but in the more platonizing sense that there is within us an inbuilt faculty whereby, apparently without divine grace, we are able to recognize and do the good. In *On Grace and Free Will*, for example, Augustine attributes, without reference to the notion of grace, considerable power to both mind or spirit and will. In modern thought, the belief is sometimes held that free choice takes place indifferently and entirely free from any determination, but in Augustine the theory of freedom derived from his inheritance from the Greek philosophical tradition, with its tendency to assume that, by virtue of the spark of divinity that defines human reason, freedom is an intrinsic possession. In that respect, too, Augustine remains the intellectual father of us all.

Those two sides of Augustine recur in different forms in the Western tradition, classically in the dispute between Luther and Erasmus, in which it is possible to see the two sources of the Christian tradition, Jerusalem and Athens, in open contention. The dispute continues to appear in new guises, for example, in secularized form in modern philosophical debate, as witness recent disputes about the compatibility of freedom and determinism. It is also important to see that at stake is rarely *merely* a question of Athens against Jerusalem, for the reason that Western debate is suffused by both traditions. That is why even the apostle of autonomy could not avoid engagement with a form of the doctrine of original sin.[3] And both views, the libertarian and the 'determinist', have much evidence in their favour.

The attraction of the libertarian position is manifest. It appears to be required by the very nature of the human being. Unless there is a kind of personal space in which we may be ourselves, and thus do what is authentically ours; unless there is space between the agent and whatever is conceived to influence or determine action, whether that be God or the world; unless it could be said that an agent could have done otherwise, what happens to the notions of freedom and responsibility? Even God, it is argued, cannot take that away without taking away anything recognizably describable as freedom.

---

[3] Gordon E. Michalson, Jr, *Fallen Freedom: Kant on Radical Evil and Moral Regeneration* (Cambridge: Cambridge University Press, 1990).

Against some aspects of this position, however, a range of arguments is arrayed. That most obviously in the tradition of the Fourth Gospel is Coleridge's form of moderate Calvinism which holds that, although there is personal space in which freedom is exercised, the space is vacated once a wrong or evil course of action is chosen. A less moderate position, and possibly the recent most philosophically sophisticated refutation of the libertarian position, is that of Jonathan Edwards, whose brilliant reductive analysis is worth reviewing briefly. Edwards argues that what he calls the Arminian notion of completely undetermined will is untenable, because all acts of will are at least in part determined by some prior factor, such as motive, conviction or argument. His is a reductive argument to the effect that sense simply cannot be made of pure libertarianism. When something is willed, he argues, it is not willed emptily, but by virtue of some reason or motive. To suppose that the will itself determines the will is to lay oneself open to various infinite regresses, unless some notion of causality operates to give a reason for the choice that the will makes.[4]

Edwards, it must be recalled, was at once an Enlightenment philosopher and a Calvinist theologian,[5] and it is the effective absence of God from most modern debate that makes the problem of the relation of determinism and freedom so resistant to solution. If the physical world and not a personal and transcendent agent is the determining agent, we seem to be left with a stark choice: either absolute freedom or absolute determinism, because it is only personal agents who can be conceived to have the capacity to enter into relations, even causal relations, with others in such a way that their freedom is preserved. Thus I can request an action of another in such a way that I can be said to cause it to be done, and yet without any coercion or overriding of autonomy. Can we say the same of my being determined to do something and yet remain free when the antecedent physical conditions of my world are supposed to be the cause, especially in view of the almost inescapable tendency of the modern mind to conceive the world mechanistically?

But here we return to the original problem. I may cause another human agent to do something without depriving him of freedom.

---

[4] Jonathan Edwards, *A Careful and Strict Enquiry into the Modern Prevailing Notions of that Freedom of the Will which is supposed to be essential to moral agency, etc.* in *The Works of Jonathan Edwards* (Banner of Truth, 1934), vol.1, pp.1-93. Strict and careful it is; much of it, I believe, is unanswerable.

[5] See especially, Robert W. Jenson, *America's Theologian: A Recommendation of Jonathan Edwards* (New York: Oxford University Press, 1988).

But I am finite. Suppose that the cause is conceived to be an infinite agent, omniscient and omnipresent, the being sometimes described in theology as 'the all-determining reality'? Here we return to the offence that the modern often takes at the very idea of God, for, rightly or wrongly, it is now often said that God has been presented in Christianity in such a way as to appear to override human moral agency. Is there any way of so conceiving the relation of God to the world that he can continue to be conceived to be the God of Christian belief — creator, reconciler and perfecter of all things — and yet not only the respecter of human freedom, but its cause? Can God the omnipotent be conceived to give what he commands, without at the same time depriving the agent of liberty, almost of reality? That is the question addressed in different ways in these papers.

II

Two papers, one largely historical, the other philosophical, will serve to set the scene. In the first, Brian Horne engages in a study of John Milton, one of the fountainheads of the modern conception of freedom, particularly as it took shape in the political realm. Though Milton was concerned in his *Areopagitica* with the freedom of the press, the content of his essay is a wrestling with the nature of freedom as it is understood through the focus provided by the Genesis account of the Fall. From one point of view, Milton's discussion replicates that of other debates in the history of Western theology, and particularly that between Augustine and Pelagius. But, as Dr Horne shows, Milton's relation to Augustine is not entirely a negative one. The poet both sees himself as standing in the Augustinian tradition, and develops an interpretation of Augustine's view of evil as the privation of good of such a kind as to suggest finally that there is no such thing as evil (p. 19).

However, the fact that Milton is fundamentally at odds with Calvinist doctrines of sin and freedom shows that in certain respects he is hostile to the heart of the thrust of Augustine's theology. To pursue a line of thought adumbrated in the previous section, we might say that Milton develops in a rather one-sided way the contribution of Athens to Augustine's thinking about freedom. The effect, argues Dr Horne, is to replicate the weakness of Pelagius, in failing to recognize the psychological complexity of the relation between knowledge and will (p. 22). Another way of putting the matter, and this emerges clearly from the argument of the paper, is that Milton's is an essentially rationalist conception of human moral action. On one interpretation of the Socratic principle that virtue is knowledge, it is impossible to sin knowingly. Truly to recognize the good is to do it. In Milton, this emerges in the view, which he shares with some Scholastic thinkers, that at the Fall reason remained untouched, so that only the will lost its capacity for good. The result is that Milton is unable to give a wholly coherent account of why the will can wilfully choose evil.

Here is to be found at once the heart of Milton's disagreement with Augustine and his characteristically modern thrust. Whereas for Augustine the Fall was *felix*, a blessed fault, because it led to a more than counterbalancing act of divine redemption, for Milton it is *felix* because it opens the way to radical freedom. 'Evil becomes an indispensable concept because it establishes the possibility of choice; it is there *necessarily,* in order that free will can be exercised' (p. 20). For us, at a time in which some of the dire consequences of that view have been experienced, all this raises one of the questions, or rather a whole set of questions, facing theologians who would on the one hand re-establish a robust conception of freedom as a gift of God, but one which cannot, on the other, be understood as Milton, and certainly his more radical successors conceived it, as an absolute possession apart from the renewal of the human relationship to God.

But before we can approach a constructive reply — we should certainly not in this realm, as in most of the topics of theology, speak of a solution — we must pass through the fire of another modern challenge, again derived from the Hellenic inheritance of the West, but also taking characteristically modern form. Stewart Sutherland's contribution to the discussion serves to represent another side of the Athenian position in the modern construal of the problem. That this is indeed the case is evidenced by the fact that he early takes an example from Greek tragedy, where matters of fate and responsibility, determinism and freedom, are so much at the centre. But significant also is his concern for self-sufficiency, what I have above described as autonomy. 'In plain terms, the question at issue is whether the self-sufficiency of human beings to pursue and achieve virtue is compromised either by the need for grace or the vulnerability to luck' (p. 26). The theological question remains open, however, because there is in this paper no equation of self-sufficiency with freedom. Moral 'bad luck' or grace may each imperil the former, but not necessarily the latter.

The enquiry about freedom is approached by an introduction of the consideration that while luck may not endanger freedom, some conceptions of grace do. Some conceptions of purposive divine action towards the moral agent may reduce freedom to an illusion; or they may render the agency of God apparently arbitrary and unjust (so argued David Hume). The solution, however, is not to seek to find the middle point in some supposed spectrum, but to supplement the thought of Hume with that of Kierkegaard.

Because the human being is a synthesis of the finite and the infinite, 'human beings [are] those whose defining characteristic is that they live constantly *sub specie aeternitatis*' (p. 31). About the nature of that eternity, the philosopher is not prepared to speculate, leaving it to the theologians to take up the challenge.

As we take up the systematic task, let us return to the (at least) double challenge presented by the previous papers: to our conceptions of freedom and to those of divine action towards the moral agent. The first of those in turn divides into two, the matter of sin and its apparent limitation or deprivation of freedom; and the character of the freedom that we may be supposed to have as persons created in the image of God. In 'Sins of Praise: The Assault on God's Freedom', Alistair McFadyen considers the implications for our topic of what is often called human fallenness. As we have seen, sin is often considered in the Christian tradition to be that which deprives of freedom, which can accordingly be restored only by the gift of God. Are we then to be conceived to be dependent upon God so radically that we not only derive our freedom from him, but are also dependent upon a personal act of restoration before we may be considered to be free? Dr McFadyen's method is to avoid the kind of attention to sin in itself that makes it of unhealthy independent interest, and rather to see it in the light of that which restores and establishes human freedom. By thus understanding it theologically, he is able to treat sin as idolatry, and so as a distortion of true human being.

'Sin is the denial of God, the refusal or blocking of proper praise' (p. 54). By resolutely refusing to consider sin except in relation to God, the author of this paper meets head on the modern secularizing accounts of the relation of divine and human, arguing that they are not only inadequate theologically, but generate views of human freedom in which we are, as free, necessarily in competition with one another. He is, to be sure, critical of the traditional construing of sin as pride, and enters into conversation, though not always agreement, with feminist critics of the notion. Both the tradition and its feminist critics fail to do justice to 'the living God of the Christian story [who] is not this kind of isolated, absolute monarch, but One who is constituted by a radical form of relation, mutuality and reciprocity ...' (p. 42). To expound this, Dr McFadyen first draws upon incarnational themes, articulating God's actual treatment of us in Christ. 'In particular, we find that the incarnation compels us to find ways of speaking of divine and human freedom as correlated ...' (p. 45).

In view of the fact, however, that the incarnation is bound up with notions of redemption, the problem of heteronomy will not yet disappear. If redemption is not to appear to involve a tearing of the fabric of human being, it must be in some way rooted in the being of the creation, in the way that God is God and the world is the world, and in particular in the form of being in relation that this implies. Thus: 'the creative and redemptive work of the triune God requires us to speak of divine presence and activity, not as space invasion, but as the creative giving of space' (p. 48). On this account, our 'freedom is to respond to God by entering into dialogue partnership' (p. 51). And so we return to the definition of sin as the refusal of the praise that this calling into relationship involves.

Much of Dr McFadyen's paper involves the rethinking, in the light of his trinitarian theology, of the notion of the human bearing of the image of God. In another paper concerned with the nature of human freedom, this comes into the centre. Christoph Schwöbel's paper, 'Imago Libertatis: Human and Divine Freedom', begins, like this Introduction, with the modern axiom that freedom is a fundamental character of the human. The first section of the paper contains an analysis of the modern development, and shows how the notion has been radicalized in recent treatments to such a degree that it not only becomes opaque in meaning, but leads to the odd situation that any discussion of freedom involves the critique of one conception of freedom by another. Building on this, Professor Schwöbel develops an analysis of freedom in terms of intentionality. This enables it to be made clear that freedom is to be discerned in many forms of action and not restricted to choices between alternatives, so that it becomes 'constitutive for what it means to be human' (p. 61). The section ends with an argument that the Kantian principle of autonomy has become in more recent times the claim that human beings constitute themselves, make themselves who they choose to be.

The second section of the paper is devoted to an analysis of the contradictory and self-destructive nature of the modern concept of freedom as self-constitution. One drawback is the inevitable disappointment of expectations and the resulting disillusionment which so unrealistic a conception generates; another, the failure to take account of the long-term consequences of our actions. The outcome is that freedom comes to appear much the same as determinism, and our quest for ourselves in effect the loss of ourselves. Modern freedom appears set on a course to lose the world also, as the environmental crisis only too well demonstrates. Freedom as self-constitution overlooks the fact 'that human agents are, as embodied agents, bound by many links into the order of the natural world' (p. 69).

In section three it is argued that the self-destructive character of modern freedom derives from the application to humanity, in the Enlightenment and its aftermath, of the late mediaeval notion of God's absolute power, power untrammelled by any limit. 'It is no accident that the most horrendous atrocities our century has seen occurred against the background of the (however misinterpreted) rhetoric of Nietzsche's superman' (p. 75). The possibilities of this analysis for a negative theology of freedom are carefully developed in the final section, whose main emphasis, however, is on a theology of positive freedom which — in contrast to a creation spirituality which fails to take account of the negative side — must be understood as a redeemed freedom. Two notions come to the fore: the notion of image not so much as imitation as transparency; and the rooting of this notion in christology. 'This freedom as transparency has as its archetype and true exemplar ... the humanity of Christ' (p. 79).

In both of the previous papers, we encountered some of the problems arising from attempts to treat freedom and its related concepts non-theologically. In other aspects of the tradition, unnecessary difficulties have been placed in the way of a theology of freedom. One of them is the notion of freedom as freedom from the law. Not only have barriers been placed in the way of a reconciliation of separated parts of the Western church by some forms of the traditional Lutheran interpretation of Paul, but the relation between faith and ethics has been unduly complicated. It sometimes appears that no ethical requirements can be placed before the believer, without suggesting that in some way 'legalism' is introduced. Francis Watson's paper takes us into the history of the interpretation of Paul, and shows among other things how influential has Luther's interpretation of Paul been on the development of modern understandings of freedom. (He shows in one footnote (n.16, p. 89), for example, that in some respects Kant's interpretation of Christianity represents a radicalized version of Luther).

Dr Watson shows that two main interpretations of Paul's understanding of freedom from the law have been determinative for mainstream interpretation. One is Jerome's view that freedom from the law means freedom from the ceremonial aspects of the Jewish tradition. This has the merit of centring on the particular context of Paul's account, something that is lost in Luther's more radical interpretation. This paper is a plea for taking the particular with complete seriousness: neither, that is to say, interpreting it in some entirely generalizing way *in despite of* its particularity, nor, in the manner of some modern theology, treating it as irrelevant *because of* that very feature.

If, then, we are prepared neither to consign Paul to some historical dustbin, nor to distort him in the interests of some modernizing theory, what might be supposed to be the significance of Paul for a modern theological understanding of freedom? Two interrelated suggestions are made. The first is that we do not treat

Paul as marooned somewhere on the other side of a great historical divide, but as linked to us through an unbroken chain of interpretation through tradition. Here, the author draws upon the important hermeneutical theories of Hans-Georg Gadamer. Second, he argues that 'the theological relevance of a Pauline text derives in part from its invitation to participate in the theological reflection that it initiated and whose basic grammatical rules it helped to establish' (p. 101). And what is chief among those rules? We expect theological significance from texts because 'Christian communal identity has already been shaped and reshaped by precisely these texts, and from the conviction that no breach in tradition has occurred that is sufficiently serious to prevent their continuing to fulfil this role in the future' (pp. 93f). Paul's central message concerns the priority of one form of communal life over another, and with that the ultimacy and universality of Jesus (p. 100).

On Dr Watson's account, a relation to Jesus through forms of communal life oriented to him is the centre of a theological conception of freedom, and his contention is linked with those of others of the papers whose authors treat God as the source of human freedom. It is here that Christian understandings come up not only against the deepest prejudices of modernity, but also into contact with some of the greatest minds of the tradition. So it is with the second of the historical papers in the collection, Ann Loades' 'Creativity, Embodiment and Mutuality: Dorothy L. Sayers on Dante, Love and Freedom.' As the title suggests, there are two focuses to her work: the influential modern writer and the mediaeval poet who meant so much to her.

The presence of studies of two such primarily literary figures in the collection reminds us that there are things to be said and ways of saying them that are closed to the merely philosophical and systematic, and so it is interesting to be reminded by Dr Loades of the importance of Christian orthodoxy as one of Miss Sayers' criteria for the adequacy of a work of art. The biographical details which are germane to an understanding of this author's work also remind us that freedom is a form of personal being and acting, and all theory and theology miss their point unless this dimension is encompassed. This does not mean that the classical intellectual difficulties involved in a discussion of God and freedom escape untreated. Two thirds of Dante's great poem, in treating purgatory and hell, raise in acute form the matter of human freedom, while this author makes it clear that both Dante and his modern interpreter faced the questions of predestination and determinism which always arise in this context, certainly in mediaeval theology.

Another dimension which returns to a recurring theme of this book is the notion that freedom is not an absolute possession of the human being, but has an end. 'If we ask Dante what freedom is for, the answer must include setting someone free for loving' (p. 109). The close link between freedom and love has other implications, of both general and contemporary theological import. What Dante 'has to say is not for Sayers marred by the tradition of Courtly Love within which he works, though for our time this will do no more than what she calls the "ecclesiastical view" of male superiority ... Her point is that human beings need to acknowledge the ways in which freedom and love may both honour one another and generously exchange places with each other on the ladder of ascent, and that the images and means of salvation may be recognized, as Dante recognized them, in both women and men' (pp. 117-18).

However, to relate freedom and love in so direct a way raises the question of the relation between divine love and human freedom. Does God's love for us set us free, and in what way? The central category by which that relation has been expressed has been that of grace, and in the final paper Colin Gunton essays a discussion of the place of that in a theology of freedom. The opening pages repeat some of the considerations introduced by Christoph Schwöbel, this time as the basis for an argument that what is required to avoid the extremes of modern conceptions is some notion of mediation. The purpose of the paper is to argue that freedom 'is not an immediate but a mediated relation to other people and the world which is the realm and object of free human action' (p. 121). There are two chief theses: that freedom should be conceived as a function of personal particularity and that the prior factor mediating freedom is the relation to God (p. 122).

The concept of grace has been vitiated in some theology by the fact that it has been conceived as a substance — like reality operating causally on human agents. The proposal of the paper is that this should be replaced by a conception of action conceived pneumatologically — as the action of God the Father mediated by God the Spirit. Such a conception enables freedom to be understood as constituted both by God and by means of patterns of relations between people. It is community that enables us to realize what we each particularly are, and that is what is meant by freedom. But this means that grace is something that characterizes — or can and should characterize — human action as well as divine.

In turn, the change of emphasis in the way grace is conceived generates a new conception of the relation between uncreated and created grace. The latter is no longer understood as a kind of substance poured into the agent, but as forms of gracious human action that the Spirit of God makes real. On such an account, freedom is the freedom to act graciously towards and receive reciprocal gracious action from our neighbour, a freedom con-

ferred by the gracious action of God the Father, realized in Christ
and through the Holy Spirit: 'For is it not a defining mark of grace
that it gives due place to the other, and therefore enables the other
to be free?' (p. 133).

2. Human Sin and Human Freedom: A Reading of Milton's *Areopagitica*

Brian Horne

It is strange to see how persistent some misconceptions about John Milton are, and stranger still to see how they are perpetuated by excellent and, otherwise reliable, scholars. Frank McConnell, for example, in his introduction to a volume of essays entitled *The Bible and the Narrative Tradition* writes of Milton: '... we can say that *Paradise Lost* is Milton's seventeenth century, Puritan midrash on the Yahwist text of the Fall, bringing that most primal of tales into synchronization with his own baroque, radical Puritan Christian interpretation of the facts of the case'[1]. Baroque? Possibly. Radical? Certainly. Puritan? Certainly not. At least not in the sense of sharing the Calvinist theology that is characteristic of English Puritanism in the seventeenth century. Milton's thinking about the story of the Fall and its consequences began much earlier in his career than *Paradise Lost*, and demonstrates a sensibility already at odds with Calvin's doctrines of sin and freedom.

In August 1644, a noted Presbyterian divine preached before the House of Commons a sermon in which he denounced the state of public morality in England. He cited a recent publication as an example of the deplorable laxity of the times: John Milton's latest shocking pamphlet on the subject of divorce. A government, he said, which permitted the propagation of such dangerous ideas needed to set its house in order immediately. 'If any plead ... for divorce for other causes than Christ and his apostles mention (of which a wicked book is abroad and uncensured, though deserving to be burnt, whose author hath been so impudent as to set his name to it and dedicate it to yourselves) ... will you grant toleration for all this'.[2] Milton did not reply immediately (as was his wont when attacked) and when he did, he did not mention

---

[1] Frank McConnell, *The Bible and the Narrative Tradition* (New York: Oxford University Press, 1986), p.11.
[2] A. N. Wilson, *The Life of John Milton* (Oxford: Oxford University Press, 1984), p.138.

divorce. That issue was already behind him. His mind was moving on another plane and in a different direction: against the Presbyterians, becoming increasingly powerful in Parliament, and against the Calvinist theology which he had previously embraced. Larger questions, precipitated by Palmer's denunciation, were now troubling him: toleration in society and the freedom of the individual.

A year earlier, in June 1643, Parliament had passed a bill for the regulation of printing and Milton had been disturbed by it, detecting an upsurge of intolerance in the growing power of the state and an attempt to curb, by force, the liberty of the individual. Palmer's sermon confirmed his misgivings. He had once believed that the overthrowing of the Crown would restore freedom to the English people; he was now aware that Presbyterian power was becoming as inquisitorial and repressive as the censorious regime of Archbishop Laud. And worse: the new masters were more zealous in their hunting down and persecution of heresies than Laud's bishops had been. At least under the old episcopal dispensation one might have managed to escape the eye of an indolent ecclesiastic, whereas now it seemed that 'the pastor of a small unlearned parish on the sudden shall be exalted archbishop over a large diocese of books, and yet not remove, but keep his other cure too, a mystical pluralist'.[3]

And so in November 1644 there appeared what many have regarded as Milton's most important prose composition, the *Areopagitica*, one of the most eloquent manifestos or an essay in political theory? Is it about sin as well as freedom? The work's ostensible purpose is to attack censorship and provide an apologia for freedom of speech; it has, thus, a practical end in view. But Milton's mind was steeped in theology and it could not address the question of the freedom of the press without, at the same time, revealing the theological foundation for the claims it was making. The *Areopagitica* may be seen as a kind of hinge in Milton's work: it opens the door backwards to show us the features of earlier phases of his intellectual career and, at the same time, opens it forwards to show us the way to future developments. Those developments will include a preoccupation with the related concepts of sin and grace, justice and freedom, that was to become central in the greatest of all his writings, *Paradise Lost*.

Many scholars have drawn attention to the place that the concept of freedom occupied in his thought. Maurice Bowra, for example, in his discussion of the complexity of the theological argument in the third book of *Paradise Lost* roundly asserts: 'At no

---

[3]   Wilson, *The Life of John Milton*, p.138.

point has he more fully emancipated himself from his earlier Calvinism than in his belief in free will'.[4] It is debatable whether Milton's thought ever accorded exactly with Calvinist teaching — especially on subjects such as free will and predestination — and by the time he came to write *Areopagitica*, it is clear that he had already embraced a formulation of the notion of freedom that was quite contrary to Calvinist anthropology. William Myers goes so far as to claim that the concept of freedom was 'the governing idea of Milton's life'.[5] His fierce defence of freedom of speech is made in the interests of political and social morality, but the concept of the freedom of speech was not, for him, as it was for many of the theorists who prepared the way for the American and French revolutions, a kind of self-evident truth: Milton's concept had a theological grounding. This is evident even when he sounds most like a Renaissance humanist.

In the treatise *On Education*, for example, he can write of his 'sanguine hopes' for human nature '... the end of learning is to repair the ruins of our first parents by regaining to know God aright'. It is a statement that could almost have come from the pen of that slightly earlier, quintessential Renaissance figure, Francis Bacon — except that Milton goes on 'and out of that knowledge, to love, to imitate him, to be like him'.[6] It is knowledge which has the power to free human beings from their bondage; it will reverse the effects of the Fall and will 'infuse into young breasts such ingenuous noble ardour, as would not fail to make many of them renowned and matchless men'.[7] We may ask if this is a kind of gnosticism, a redemption by knowledge? Almost, except that knowledge is not esoteric. But nothing is said here of the work of Christ, and sin is not discussed. But five months later came the *Areopagitica* in which the theological root can be clearly perceived: the connection between human sin and human freedom is briefly but conspicuously demonstrated. This root was to flower, twenty years later, in the great tree of *Paradise Lost*.

The crucial passage occurs about a third of the way into the essay, but before that is examined, note should be taken of one of the more famous statements which comes earlier and which is pregnant with theological significance. After an address to the Lords and the Commons in which the author begs them to recall

---

4   C. M. Bowra, *From Virgil to Milton* (London: Macmillan, 1945), p.216.
5   William Myers, *Milton and Free Will: An Essay in Criticism and Philosophy* (Andover: Croom Helm, 1987), p.6.
6   John Milton, *Selected Prose* edited by C. A. Patrides (London: Penguin Books, 1974), p.182.
7   Milton, *Selected Prose*, p. 187.

the democracy of Athens, he reminds them of their ordinance of the previous year to regulate printing: 'That no book, pamphlet or paper shall be henceforth Printed, unlesse the same be first approved and licensed by such' i.e. Parliament. The *Areopagitica* itself was an illegal tract: it had not been licensed or approved by Parliament and though Milton boldly put his own name on the title page he did not identify his printer or bookseller. He writes:

> Books are not absolutely dead things, but doe contain a potencie of life in them to be as active as that soule was whose progeny they are; nay they do preserve as in a viol the purest efficacie and extraction of that living intellect that bred them ... as good almost kill a Man as kill a good Book; who kills a Man kills a reasonable creature, God's image; but hee who destroys a good Booke, kills reason itself, kills the image of God, as it were in the eye.[8]

It is the last sentence that is interesting, and the anthropology, the doctrine of man, which is expressed in it. Granted that the treatise is polemical, the theology undergirding it is unmistakable. When Milton speaks about the human being and tries to identify what it is that makes us human, he focuses upon the capacity to reason. Here in this tract at this moment of supplication Reason is identified with the image of God; the unique quality which human beings possess and which sets them above the rest of the material creation is Reason. This notion is an ancient one. It is expounded at length, for example, by Augustine at the beginning of the fifth century in the text that Milton knew best, the *City of God*; and had become almost part of the official teaching of the Catholic Church since the time of Thomas Aquinas. Furthermore, it became the coping stone for the anthropology of the deistic interpretations of Christianity in the Renaissance. It is true that the Reformers of the sixteenth century had moved away from it, at least in its more explicit forms, but even Calvin found it difficult to reject it entirely. Milton grasps it firmly and unapologetically, and with it notions of human sin and human freedom that are far removed from the Presbyterian theology which he had earlier espoused but which he came increasingly to dislike. It is curious, however, to note that he nonetheless seemed to have believed that his own theology was in accord with Augustine's — as he tried to demonstrate several years later in *De Doctrina Christiana*.

In the Fall, Milton maintains, Reason remains untouched; what is affected is the capacity for acting upon truths supplied by Reason. In the *City of God*, Augustine had written that in the Fall

8   Milton, *Selected Prose*, pp.200-1.

human nature had become vitiated and diminished, no longer capable of sustaining supernatural communion with God; lacking the gifts of integrity, beauty, virtue and immortality. Like Augustine, Milton accepts the concept of the loss of these gifts and the Augustinian definition of Original Sin as privation, but he insists more vigorously than Augustine that something of the divine image remains and argues that natural virtue is still possible in human beings. The loss of the gifts of beauty and immortality was the loss of something 'befitting to his nature' but not the loss of something originally proper i.e. intrinsic to it. Consequently, the loss of these gifts was the loss of something strictly supernatural and did not affect what was natural. Free will and Reason both fell into this latter category — of things intrinsic to nature which were not lost in the Fall.

Tillyard's observation that in the *Areopagitica* Milton 'definitely adopts the doctrine of free-will and thus turns against the predestination of the Presbyterians' teaching'[9] may be correct, but it does not take us far enough. What are the characteristics of free will? How does it issue in action? Augustine had usually characterized sin as a deliberate act of the will i.e. the wilful rejection of the known truths of God; and Milton in *Paradise Lost* portrays the actions of Adam and Eve in eating the fruit of the forbidden tree in precisely these terms: the wilful rejection of what is known to be the command of God; and wilful in the sense of being free — not under any kind of constraint. A rather troubling question begins to surface: if the will is uncorrupt and free, why does it deliberately choose evil? And, of course, if it is perverted, or even in a state of vitiation, is it free? Unlike Maurice Bowra, I am not persuaded that Milton ever managed to enunciate a wholly coherent notion of the freedom of the will or even formed a clear picture of how it operated in making choices for good or evil. His ambivalence is apparent even in the place where one would expect him to be at his most systematic in his discussions of the teachings of the Christian Faith: *De Doctrina Christiana*.[10]

In the middle of his polemic in the *Areopagitica*, Milton turns to the story of the Fall in the third chapter of the Book of Genesis. The discussion is not extensive, but of great importance:

> Good and evill we know in the field of this World grow up together almost inseparably; and the knowledge of good is so

---

9   E. M. W. Tillyard, *Milton* (London: Penguin Books, revised edition, 1966), p. 133.

10   See an illuminating discussion of his theology in *De Doctrina Christiana* by Peter Fiore, *Milton and Augustine: Patterns of Augustinian Thought in Milton's Paradise Lost* (Penn State University Press, 1981).

involv'd and interwoven with the knowledge of evill, and in so
many cunning resemblances hardly to be discern'd, that those
confused seeds which were impos'd on *Psyche* as an incessant
labour to cull out, and sort asunder, were not more intermixt. It
was from out the rinde of one apple tasted, that the knowledge
of good and evill as two twins cleaving together leapt forth into
the World. And perhaps this is the doom which Adam fell into
of knowing good and evill, that is to say of knowing good by evill.
As therefore the state of man now is; what wisdom can there be
to choose, what continence to forbeare without the knowledge of
evill? He that can apprehend and consider vice with all her baits
and seeming pleasures, and yet abstain, and yet distinguish,
and yet prefer that which is truly better, he is the true warfaring
Christian.[11]

Tillyard's commentary on this passage reads as follows: 'Man is
born with the seeds of good and evil in him: here environment
cannot determine his character; in the most favourable environment evil might come out. But man has the power of choice, and
knowing both good and evil it is possible for him to choose good.
The present world may not ever be perfect but it may be very much
better. It is reasonable to have very high hopes ... There is
therefore every incentive for the noblest and most strenuous
action.'[12] There is an ambiguity in the exposition which needs to be
investigated: who, exactly, is this 'man' that Tillyard is referring
to? Is it us — our ruined race, fallen, in the state of Original Sin?
Or is it, perhaps, unfallen humanity, Adam and Eve? And if that
is the case, is a thesis being offered in which the unfallen creation
is seen as already possessing within it good and evil? Are these, so
to speak, ontological entities? If that is what is being proposed
what are we to make of the refrain in the opening chapter of the
Book of Genesis that God looked upon all that he had made and
'behold it was very good'? Tillyard does not address these questions, but before dismissing him for not seeing the theological
implications of his assertions, we must ask whether there is not a
corresponding ambiguity in the text of the *Areopagitica* itself.[13]

Milton sees himself as standing in the Augustinian tradition;
and as he interprets Augustine he sees Adam and Eve in their
original state not knowing good, as we do, by separating it from

[11] Milton, *Selected Prose*, pp.212-13.
[12] Tillyard, *Milton*, p.137.
[13] Denis Saurat goes so far as to suggest that Milton saw the whole
      creation as being divine and tries to solve the problem of the existence
      of evil by resorting to a Rosicrucian notion which obliterates the
      distinction between good and evil. Denis Saurat, *Milton: Man and
      Thinker* (London: J. M. Dent, 1944).

evil in a dualistic way. Milton's universe is wholly monistic in conception: everything proceeds in perfection *de Deo*; Adam and Eve are part of the Good: it can be said that there is no such thing as evil. According to Augustine evil had no real existence: it is known only in relation to the good i.e. as the absence of the good: *privatio boni*. It is possible to choose the absence of good, evil, but that, in essence, is the choice to know something in a particular way: a state of being that exists only in and for the will that chooses it. All knowledge in itself is good, according to Milton; but there can be a way of knowing that is evil. He seems to be talking here about two different modes of apprehension — as indicated by that strange phrase: to 'know good by evil'. As there can be no evil to know, in the ontological sense (for evil has no ontology), we can only will to know the good in a perverted manner. In an earlier passage he has already announced that knowledge in itself, whether of good or evil, cannot corrupt: '... To the pure all things are pure, not only meats and drinks, but all kinds of knowledge whether of good or evill; the knowledge cannot defile, nor consequently the books, if the will and conscience be not defil'd.'[14]

Inasmuch as he locates the sin of Adam in the disobedience to the known command of God, he is offering an orthodox interpretation of the Genesis story. Like many Patristic theologians he seems to think that the command was, in any case, merely arbitrary. Peter Fiore is surely correct in his comment on the theological discourses of the eighth book of *Paradise Lost* that 'Milton's God did not say "Thou shalt not ask too many questions about the solar system or the sex life of angels". He said, in speaking of the Tree of Knowledge "Remember what I warn thee, shun to taste/And shun the bitter consequence".'[15] Does it matter that this tree is called the tree of the knowledge of good and evil? If the command of God is purely arbitrary, it could have been a prohibition against anything at all. And, indeed in *De Doctrina* this is what he does argue, but not in the *Areopagitica*; and so he moves the argument on: to consider the nature of the prohibition in relation to that which is prohibited: the tree which is specifically, and perhaps not arbitrarily, designated as the tree of the knowledge of good and evil.

Here we reach the centre of Milton's thought on sin and freedom in the *Areopagitica*; and we have to consider whether he had, by this time, become so wedded to the notion of free will and so committed to safeguarding the centrality of its position in his anthropology that he saw evil not merely as an inescapable fact of human experience, but a necessary fact of God's creation: '... what

[14] Milton, *Selected Prose*, p.211.
[15] Fiore, *Milton and Augustine*, p.40.

wisdome can there be to choose, what continence to forbeare
without the knowledge of evill? ...' Evil becomes an indispensable
concept because it establishes the possibility of choice; it is there
necessarily, in order that free will can be exercised. That is how
Milton lays the foundation for his theodicy: he does not begin with
the fact of evil and view it as a problem to be solved in relation to
the justice, power and love of God, he begins with the fact of human
freedom and proceeds to argue for the existence of evil as a
necessary means by which this freedom can be exercised. So, for
him, it becomes impossible to conceive of freedom without simultaneously thinking of evil as well as good. It could be said, in
consequence, that the Fall becomes a necessary and inevitable
occurrence (whether one speaks of it historically or mythologically)
if the human being is to be truly human i.e. free. He or she must,
it seems, know good only by knowing evil otherwise he or she
cannot choose the good. There is, one might say, truly a *felix culpa*;
though the *culpa* of Adam and Eve is not *felix* because it brings
about redemption by the Incarnation of the Son of God (as it would
be in Augustine's interpretation of the Fall); it is *felix* because it
opens the way to radical freedom. 'Granted the choice between
unconscious good in mindless immortality and a period of wisdom
followed by death, Milton would choose the latter.'[16] The fortunate
Fall becomes the virtuous Fall.

Is this a coherent theory, or is Milton falling into a logical trap?
The human being (Adam and Eve) must already be aware of the
possibility of choosing evil if he or she knowingly rebels against the
command of God in eating of the fruit of the free. The fruit,
therefore, cannot, logically, be said to confer the knowledge of good
and evil — as is plainly stated in the Genesis story. This leads
Christopher Kendrick to argue, with some justification, that
Milton did not see that if Adam and Eve were created with the
capacity of exercising free will in the way that has been described,
'it is not too much to say that they are framed by creation to fall ...
that they are already fallen from the moment of their first
appearance'.[17] And if this is the case, it logically must follow that
in Milton's theology there can be no place for either the doctrine of
Original Righteousness or that of Original Sin. Kendrick does not
actually drive his argument through to its logical conclusion: I am
extrapolating this conclusion from the dilemma which Kendrick
has indicated.

[16] W. B. C. Watkins, *An Anatomy of Milton's Verse* (Baton Rouge, 1955),
      p.131.
[17] Christopher Kendrick, *Milton: A Study in Ideology and Form* (London:
      Methuen, 1986), p.215.

It is clear from what came later in his career that Milton did not believe, and indeed could not believe, that he had painted himself into this corner: except that in the closing pages of *Paradise Lost*, written two decades later, an ambiguity is suggested about the state of the two human creatures. Is it happy or unhappy?

> They looking back, all th' Eastern side beheld
> Of Paradise, so late their happie seat,
> Wav'd over by that flaming Brand, the Gate
> With dreadful Faces throng'd and fierie Armes:
> Som natural tears they drop'd, but wip'd them soon;
> The World was all before them, where to choose
> Thir place of rest, and Providence thir guide:
> They hand in hand with wandring steps and slow,
> Through *Eden* took thir solitarie way. (12.641-9)

A fine mesh is woven: of sadness and hope: a vibration of loss and tremor of expectation. The life before them seems to offer so much more than the grim picture painted by the Lord in the Genesis story.

I do not think that Milton ever resolved the problem he had created and provided a coherent theory of the relation of human freedom to human sin because he never related the concepts of knowledge and will satisfactorily. In the fifth book of *Paradise Lost*, Eve tells Adam of a disturbing dream she has had. In comforting her Adam replies:

> Yet evil whence? in thee can harbour none,
> Created pure.
> ... Evil into the mind of God or Man
> May come and go, so unapprov'd, and leave
> No spot or blame behind: Which gives me hope
> That what in sleep thou didst abhorr to dream
> Waking thou never wilt consent to do. (5.99ff.)

As C. S. Lewis has pointed out, 'the whole point of Adam's speech seems to be that the approval of the will alone makes a mind evil and that the presence of evil as an object of thought does not';[18] hence, evil dreams which, by definition, are *un*willed, can effect nothing: they are the children of, what Milton calls Fancy. It seems that humanity is equipped with the capacity to contemplate

[18] C. S. Lewis, *A Preface to Paradise Lost* (Oxford: Oxford Paperbacks, 1960), p.84.

serenely both good and evil without desiring one or the other. The will is brought into play after the alternatives have been duly considered. This does not contradict what had been implied in the *Areopagitica*, but there is a shift in focus. In the earlier work Milton was trying to answer the question, how do we know that something is good? What is it that we are recognizing when we describe something as good? His answer is that we know good by knowing its opposite; that we recognize something as being good only when we have separated it from evil. Here in *Paradise Lost* his focus, however briefly, is on the will. As in the earlier works he propounds the thesis that knowledge itself, of whatever kind, cannot cause harm and that we can know evil without having to choose it; there is no 'leaning' towards it, no innate propensity towards it. Like many theologians in the Christian tradition he wants to locate human sin in the act of intention, the will. There is, moreover, for him, no exterior supernatural cause of this sin — no one forced Adam and Eve to act in the way they did despite the blandishments of Satan in the Garden of Eden — it is the individual human being who is personally responsible for deliberate acts of wickedness, freely chosen.

Milton has moved a long way, theologically, from the Calvinism of the seventeenth century in this treatment of sin and freedom. It is the rejection of a doctrine of Original Sin adumbrated by St Paul and developed by Augustine in the fourth century and Calvin in the sixteenth; and it is open to the criticism that Augustine made of Pelagius' theory of sin and freedom in the early years of the fifth century: a failure to recognize the psychological complexity of the relation between knowledge and will in every human decision. We may even want, in the manner of some forms of Catholic theology, to retain a strong emphasis on a concept of free will and still find Milton's account unsatisfactory. C. S. Lewis tried to defend Milton on this point in *A Preface to Paradise Lost*: '... our own common sense tells us that we no more become bad by thinking of badness than we become triangular by thinking about triangles'.[19] But Lewis, here, fails to distinguish between the different kinds of knowledge that human beings are capable of and deliberately confuses moral and mathematical knowledge. Knowledge of the distinction between good and evil (as J. H. Newman was at pains to point out in the *Grammar of Assent*) is categorically different from knowledge of the distinction between a triangle and a square. Milton makes the same confusion: he asserts that all knowledge is received and appropriated in the same way; furthermore it is unrelated to the will. Milton seems to have rejected the

[19] Lewis, *Preface*, p.84.

cry of St Paul in his letter to the Romans: 'the good I would do I do not do, and the evil I would not do, that I do'. It was a statement which imprinted itself upon the Christian imagination and which became a kind of existential expression of the doctrine of Original Sin. Milton seems to have believed that all knowledge was 'intellectual' knowledge; that evil could be known in the abstract — a theory that the story of the Fall in the Book of Genesis seems specifically to contradict. The myth of Adam and Eve and their disobedience implies that, for mankind, knowledge of evil is inseparable from experience of its consequences: existential as well as intellectual. This is one of the pivotal points of Denis Saurat's interpretation of *Paradise Lost*; that it was an intellectual error, brought about by Satan's keen sophistry, that caused the fall of Adam and Eve; they were acting on the basis of erroneous information. Milton becomes, in this interpretation, a kind of seventeenth-century gnostic. If this were true, Milton's theodicy would have been more coherent, but viewing his work as a whole, we find no absolutely consistent theory of freedom and sin. He refuses both the neat symmetry of gnosticism and the integrity of classical Calvinism. He was clearly attracted to the idea of salvation by knowledge, but close examination of the latter work shows that he was not, in the end, persuaded that the deepest mysteries of the human condition could be revealed and dealt with by the diligent application of the rational faculty.

In the *Areopagitica* he came as close as he ever came to believing in salvation by knowledge and the absolute freedom of the human being to choose between good and evil on the basis of intellectual information; and we can see why, in his hatred of prejudice and intolerance, he took this line. It marked the climax of a movement of thought and action which had begun seven years before: it ended one phase and began another. Both *Paradise Lost* and *Samson Agonistes* move away from the theological perspective of the *Areopagitica*, and when he came to deal with these questions of human sin and human freedom he was able to let the complexity of poetry carry the perplexity of his theological imaginings: '... the poem asks from us, at one and the same time, two incompatible responses ... that Adam did right, and ... that he did wrong. The dilemma is as critical as that, and there is no way of escape'.[20] This ambivalence is created and sustained not only by the mastery of Milton's poetic characterization, but also by his theology of Original Sin itself and his interpretation of the Fall: the seeds of which he was sowing twenty years earlier in the *Areopagitica*.

---

[20] A. J. Waldock, *Paradise Lost and its Critics* (Cambridge: Cambridge University Press, 1947), p.56.

3. God and Freedom

Stewart R. Sutherland

In the sixteenth century, a man called John Bradford, watching criminals being led to execution, uttered the often misquoted words: 'But for the grace of God, there goes John Bradford.' These words could be understood in a variety of ways, and an exploration of the richness implicit in them will provide a convenient starting point for this paper. However, before I begin that exploration, there is one fundamental point to be made to which I shall return on more than one occasion; our starting point, and indeed our conclusions, have to do with the ways in which men and women perceive themselves in the midst of life.

Bradford's response to the mixture of fate and misery which he saw before him has many elements to it, but the first to note is undoubtedly a proper sense of humility in the face of those condemned by the judicial process. Negatively, the implication for our topic is that we find in this uncomplicated reaction of a believer the religious version of a secular view put more formally by Bernard Williams' historical reflection:

> The idea that one's whole life can in some ... way be rendered immune to luck has perhaps rarely prevailed ... (it did not prevail, for instance, in mainstream Christianity). [1]

As Martha Nussbaum's most important study of this issue in *The Fragility of Goodness* [2] shows, there was a preoccupation in Greek intellectual life with the relationship between happiness and fortune. Was it just, in Williams' terms, bad 'luck', or in Shakespeare's, one of 'the slings and arrows of outrageous fortune' which lay at the foundation of Oedipus' future misery? That chance meeting with a cantankerous old man at the crossing of the ways was surely against the odds as a meeting, let alone a meeting with an estranged and unrecognized father? The literary device

---

[1] See 'Moral Luck' in the book of that title, by Bernard Williams (Cambridge: Cambridge University Press, 1981) p.20.
[2] Martha Nussbaum, *The Fragility of Goodness* (Cambridge: Cambridge University Press, 1986), ch. 1.

which introduces Sophocles' tragedy is in that respect at least not unlike in function a comparably chance encounter in Tom Wolfe's *Bonfire of the Vanities*.[3]

In each case, with varying cultural signals, men and women of vigour and apparent self-sufficiency have comparable fundamental questions raised about the limits of their self-sufficiency. Of course, the differences are greater, both in the writing and in the portrayal of character, and doubtless the element of envious 'serves him right too' mentality in the response of many to the demise of Wolfe's Sherman McCoy is not likely to have been dominant in Sophocles' audiences. Nonetheless the chill which is prompted in the minds of some who respond to the themes of Wolfe, bears some analogy to that felt by those who still today are disturbed by the myths of ancient Greece out of which Sophocles constructed tragedy. The link which they have to the metaphorical drawing of breath reflected in Bradford's words 'but for the grace of God', is that they *question* individual human self-sufficiency.

I

These opening remarks are offered as a context which will allow us to define more clearly which of the myriad of questions which could be raised under the intellectual generosity of the title will in fact be tackled in this paper. The connections to be made are as follows. If human beings are to have the freedom not simply to pursue, but deliberately to achieve, goals, then that implies a degree of self-sufficiency. In the secular terms within which Williams discusses these matters, what is necessary is the relevant immunity to (bad) luck. Williams, as he makes plain, is sceptical about the validity of the belief that we do have that kind of autonomy:

> One's history as an agent is a web in which anything that is the product of the will is surrounded and held up and partly formed by things that are not, in such a way that reflection can go only in one of two directions: either in the direction of saying that responsible agency is a fairly superficial concept, which has a limited use in harmonizing what happens, or else that it is not a superficial concept, but that it cannot ultimately be purified.[4]

The first point here is clear and I shall return to the theological implications of the second later in the paper.

In theological terms, the 'immunity' in question would have to be

---

[3] Tom Wolfe, *The Bonfire of the Vanities* (London: Jonathan Cape, 1988).
[4] Williams, *Moral Luck*, p.29.

provided by the fateful intervention of an active God, whether in terms of the dark purposiveness implied at the conclusion of Thomas Hardy's *Tess of the D'Urbevilles:* 'the President of the Immortals ... ended his sport with Tess ...', or in terms of the absence of any necessity for the grace of a God for which John Bradford was so evidently thankful. Kant's version of this is summed up in the slogan attributed to him 'ought implies can'. The responsibility to pursue virtue presupposes the possibility of achieving virtue. In terms of our discussion, if we ought to be virtuous, then we must presuppose the degree of self-sufficiency necessary to repel 'the slings and arrows' — that is to say the self-sufficiency necessary for immunity to luck and fortune and the self-sufficiency which sees grace as an unnecessary or morally ennervating intrusion. In plain terms, the question at issue is whether the self-sufficiency of human beings to pursue and achieve virtue is compromised either by the need for grace or the vulnerability to luck.

There are several points to be made here of which the first is that even if we have a duty to pursue virtue, that does not mean that we have a duty to achieve virtue, and that while self-sufficiency may be required for the latter (achieving virtue) it is not *ipso facto* necessary for the former, the pursuit of virtue. What is necessary for the former is a certain degree of freedom. Hence vulnerability to luck or fortune does compromise human self-sufficiency, but does not inevitably compromise human freedom. One theological question is whether there is a parallel here between fortune/luck and grace in both respects. That is to say, there is no doubt that vulnerability to fortune or luck sets limits to human self-sufficiency but not necessarily to human freedom if freedom is taken to be the freedom to pursue rather than to achieve virtue. There is also no doubt that the need for grace also implies a limit to human self-sufficiency, but does it also follow that the need for grace sets limits to human freedom?

The second issue arising relates to this. Bernard Williams' conclusion about the vulnerability of self-sufficiency to luck is that the moral is not 'supreme', not genuinely unconditional.[5] The implied theological question is whether the limits set to self-sufficiency and/or freedom by the need for grace set limits also to the moral, to the obligation either to pursue or to achieve virtue. I shall return to this question, which is the most fundamental which I wish to pose, in due course.

II

The force of my argument so far is to raise the question of whether

---

[5] Williams, *Moral Luck*, pp.37-8.

the constraints put upon our conception of morality in a non-theological context by the sort of analysis of moral luck offered by Bernard Williams can be transposed to comparable constraints set by the theological concept of grace, and the human need for it implied in John Bradford's quoted remark. The answer to that question is, I believe, that there are significant differences. The fact that they both limit our belief in self-sufficiency does not imply that they are logically on all fours with respect to freedom. The situation, however, is complex. Vulnerability to luck or fortune, I have argued, does not compromise freedom to pursue virtue, but it does compromise freedom to achieve virtue. In the case of grace, I shall argue that the answer to the question of whether grace implies limits to freedom to pursue virtue, as well as limits to the human self-sufficiency to achieve virtue, depends upon the account which we give of grace.

The varieties possible here are considerable in number but I want to suggest that each variation in the possible account which we might give of grace will lie on a spectrum between two limiting cases. At one end of the spectrum, the account given of the rôle of grace in the world of human purpose and action will differ little from talk of an impersonal working out of fortune, whether outrageous or not, which differs little from what we have been referring to as 'moral luck'. Thus: But for the absence of outrageous fortune, there goes John Bradford. In that extreme and impersonal account of grace, there is no implied constraint in John Bradford's freedom to pursue virtue, although ill-fortune may deprive him of successful achievement of that virtue.

The price, however, of removing the tension between the concept of grace and the pursuit of virtue is so to modify the concept of grace that its effects seem little different from the effects of a random and mechanistic throwing of dice. That rain should fall equally unpurposively upon the just and the unjust as an element of our perception of grace may leave us as free to pursue virtue as when confronted by Shakespeare's slings and arrows, but it does not leave us with much of a concept of grace. Of course, however, we must remind ourselves that this particular account of grace (if such it be) is an ultimate limiting conception at one furthest end of the spectrum, and is hardly therefore a real test of the effectiveness of the concept. I do accept this point, but before moving to the other end of the spectrum, I do wish to underline the fact that at this end of the spectrum freedom to pursue virtue and therefore the responsibility to pursue virtue are not compromised. Let us consider the account which might be given of the concept at the opposing extremity of the spectrum.

To sketch such an account we substitute the personal for the impersonal and the purposive for the mechanistic. This strengthens and enriches the concept of grace immensely by implying a source of the effects of grace which is quite different from the 'source' of outrageous fortune's slings and arrows. Thus for the paraphrase: *But for the absence of outrageous fortune, there goes John Bradford*, we can substitute the following expansion: *But for the action of a personal and purposive God, there goes John Bradford*. Now this has the theological advantage of giving a distinctive account of grace which is certainly not in danger of being confused with fortune, whether outrageous or not. However, there are disadvantages. Two of these relate to the difficulties which arise for our grasp of what freedom to pursue virtue amounts to, and two to the implied concept of God.

The first of these difficulties is whether or not we have in fact only the illusion of freedom, and if this fear is well-grounded, then this conception of the grace of God sets the greatest possible limit to our freedom to pursue virtue. If there be such a God, and if such a God may choose either to act or not to act graciously, then are we merely the small children in the garden, believing ourselves to be freely working out purposes of significance and taking final responsibility for these purposes; or are all of our deeds and purposes subject in the end to the constraints set by and potential intervention of those who know better what is good for us? In such a case, freedom to pursue virtue, which must include freedom to set and pursue specific goals, is deeply in question.

The second related difficulty also concerning our concept of freedom is raised by the very idea of a purposive and gracious God. If such a gracious purposive being exists, how much freedom do we have within his purposes? Is it sufficient to formulate moral goals and to pursue them? If so, why is that apportioning of freedom not sufficient to achieve those goals? Or if it is sufficient what need do we have of the (interventionist) grace of God? If God's grace is to be seen in the initial provision of freedom, rather than in some interventionist form ('special' grace), then why is that grace relevant to the distinction between John Bradford and the criminals whom he observed?

The difficulties raised by this account of grace for the concept of God are well-known and closely correlated to the above points about freedom. All of these points were made most effectively by Hume in his *Dialogues Concerning Natural Religion*[6] and therefore I shall note rather than dwell upon them. The first is that such

---

[6]   David Hume, *Dialogues Concerning Natural Religion*, edited by Norman Kemp Smith, (Edinburgh: Thomas Nelson, 1947).

a gracious purposive God seems to be rather selective in his interventions. Why should John Bradford have the support of the grace of God, but apparently not so the poor wretches who provoked the chilled *frisson* in his heart? The second difficulty is that if we depend upon appeal to concepts such as purposiveness and personalness to distinguish the grace of God from 'slings and arrows', then the logic of the situation is that we give content to the distinction by increasing the anthropomorphism and Philo's reminder to Cleanthes is relevant. The force of the distinction is stronger, the closer the analogy between divine purposiveness and human purposiveness. Weaken the comparison, and you diminish the cogency of the argument:

> Now Cleanthes, said Philo, with an air of alacrity and triumph, mark the consequences. *First,* by this method of reasoning you remove all claims to infinity in any of the attributes of deity ...
>
> *Secondly,* you have no reason, on your Theory, for ascribing perfection to the Deity ...[7]

Summary

The general point which I am making in this section of the paper is that concepts of the grace of God may be developed on a wide spectrum of options. At one end of the spectrum, such a concept does not cause any more difficulties for the notion of human freedom to pursue virtue, than does the equivalent non-theological idea of fortune or luck. The price, however, is that there seems to be little difference then between talk of grace and talk of luck and John Bradford might have thanked his lucky stars as much as the grace of God. At the other end of the spectrum, however, where grace is differentiated from luck by the language of personhood and purposiveness, then difficulties are raised for both the concept of freedom and the concept of God.

Where do we go from here? We could stress that these are accounts of the grace of God at the opposite ends of the spectrum and that it may be possible to develop a more subtle account somewhere in the middle of the spectrum which can exist in tension with a more subtle account of freedom. If there are those who wish to pursue such an intellectual path, I wish them luck, or supporting grace, depending on their point of view. However, I wish to point the argument in a rather different direction.

---

[7]   Hume, *Dialogues*, Section 5.

III

The conceptions of grace, albeit two opposing cases on a spectrum, and the view of the slings and arrows of outrageous fortune, have two points in common. In the first place, they all recognize the limits of human perceptions of and aspirations to self-sufficiency. The second is that they do so by contrasting what I can only call the finite and the infinite. Thus in trying to think within the limits of human finitude, those who see those limits spelt out in adversity can help deal with that perception either by thrusting adversity or its origins onto some alternative non-purposive plane which impinges on our own in random fashion — luck or fortune — or by seeking protection against the effects of such adversity through some non-finite source of grace.

In each case, the implied picture or perception of human life ('definition' is too strong a word) is to identify its core with the finite and its purposes with goals which are definable within this finite temporal world. In the appropriate ideal conception of human life our self-sufficiency would be such as to render the achievement of those goals as falling well within human competence. Where we fail we 're-position' ourselves through the language of 'bad luck' if we are prosaic or 'the slings and arrows of outrageous fortune' if we are not. To overcome the pessimistic implications of such a new perception of ourselves, we may begin to talk and perhaps in some sense believe in the language of the grace of God. Even if we do not overtly fail, we may have the insight of the John Bradfords of this world to realize that we do not all as human beings live on a level moral playing-field, and therefore be thankful for the grace of God.

These different ways of talking, 'grace', 'luck', 'fortune', do each help with the perception of ourselves as lacking the self-sufficiency of the gods, of the President of the Immortals (Hardy) or of the Masters of the Universe (Wolfe). As such they serve us partially well, but they do so at a cost. The cost is that they set us in a world defined and limited by that way of talking where the limits of those particular perceptions of self-sufficiency are the limits of the finite temporal world.

There are two ways to question this which are complementary to one another. The first is to try to re-formulate accounts of human purposiveness which are not defined by those particular perceptions of self-sufficiency. The second is to give an account of human beings which does not assume that our position is essentially that of finite human beings in an alien infinite world. Kierkegaard offers us a starting point here in his characterization of a 'genuine human being' as 'a synthesis of the finite and the infinite', who 'finds his reality in holding these two factors together'.[8]

Alternatively, it might be argued, this is the perception of human beings as those whose defining characteristic is that they live constantly *sub specie aeternitatis*. As such they are essentially pilgrims or travellers aware of the limits of self-sufficiency implied in their ambiguous status, but equally aware that their ignorance (lack of omniscience) leaves room for the freedom necessary to pursue goals, to formulate purposes whose achievement is by no means guaranteed.

The contrast which I wish to highlight is this: the approaches to the questions raised and discussed in the Introduction and Sections I and II of the paper imply a perception of human life, and the freedom to pursue virtue as wholly bounded by the finite. Luck, fortune or grace in their various ways, both set limits to human aspirations to self-sufficiency and imply that the even finite tenor of our ways is subject to the interaction between what we to some extent effect or control the finite and the infinite which does not fall under our influence. Kierkegaard's proposal is to perceive or understand ourselves as existing in tension between 'a synthesis of' finite and infinite.[9]

8   Søren Kierkegaard, *Concluding Unscientific Postscript*, translated by D. F. Swenson and W. Lowrie, (Princeton: Princeton University Press 1941), p.268.
9   I have developed some of these themes more fully in *God, Jesus and Belief* (Oxford: Blackwell, 1984).

4. Sins of Praise: The Assault on God's Freedom

Alistair McFadyen

I. Introduction

One of the underlying assumptions that I am going to work with is that sin is an essentially theological language. That is to say, the language of sin functions by referring a situation to God, indicating how the distortion, brokenness and wickedness found there constitute a denial and contradiction of God's presence, activity and will. Where the reference to God is lost through translation into a secular (say, moral) language, there the language of sin ceases to have any effective function; and it ceases to do so precisely because it now fails to relate God to the world. God-talk is collapsed into a secular discourse which, it is supposed, is a more adequate way of explaining and understanding what is wrong with the world. We might try to baptize secular ways of diagnosing, explaining and conceptualizing what is wrong, by tacking talk of God onto the analysis given to us and naming as 'sin' that which it identifies as problematic. But we cannot change the fact that here the world is being explained without God; that here God is a redundant hypothesis with no explanatory power when it comes to understanding the world and our situation in it. If it is believed that talk of God's presence and activity has no explanatory power in relation to the world, then it is hard to see the integrity of continuing to use the language of sin at all. If one is going to give up on God, one ought to give up on the language of sin. Alternatively, if the language of sin is to be retained as having some explanatory power which cannot be expropriated by discourses which exclude God, that can only be by maintaining an explicit and primary reference to God's presence and activity.

We have arrived at something like a grammatical rule for using the language of sin through the formal recognition of sin as a theological language: that reference to God must be explicitly built into it, not elided. But this is not yet adequate for ruling specifically Christian use of the language of sin, since it refers not to the specific character of the Christian God, but to God in the abstract. So Christian use of the language of sin has to have inbuilt reference to the Christian God: the triune God who loves in freedom.

What are the implications of all this for the theme of sin and freedom? First, that we are only justified in considering freedom together with sin if that freedom is either God's or else is rooted in God. It is only permissible to speak of freedom in relation to sin if freedom is somehow related to the Christian God. If we fail to meet this condition, then the result will almost certainly be a discussion of human freedom with no intrinsic reference to God, which consequently features as self-defining and as self-constituting. The danger of collapsing God-talk into talking about ourselves without reference to God can be avoided by making talk of God primary. In relation to sin, we first have to talk of God before we talk about ourselves as a means of ensuring that the reference to God remains intact even, or rather especially, in our self-descriptions and analyses.

It is the contention of this paper that sin may best be defined as an assault on God; or, better, as an assault on God's freedom. If that is the case, then a discussion of freedom will be very much to the heart of a Christian conception of sin. But the freedom we primarily have to do with in relation to sin is God's, not our own. So when we speak of sin, reference to God's freedom must be primary; reference to human freedom, secondary.

Now, I realize that this will look as if I am set to deny any positive content or function to human freedom; worse, to define the exercise of human freedom as itself sinful. Why so? Because we have been culturally attuned to regard divine and human freedom as competitive. Hence we are caught in the following dilemma: we either acknowledge God's sovereign freedom, in which case we must reject our freedom, prostrate ourselves and become God's puppets or slaves; or else we can assert our own freedom in a rebellion of Promethean *hubris* over against God. We are presented with the dichotomy between autonomy, being one's own law-giver, and heteronomy, obeying the laws of a God who is transcendent Other, and therefore alien to our being.

II. Freedom and Sin Misconstrued

The misconception of freedom

This understanding of freedom is, I believe, misconceived. At its root lies a way of thinking about transcendence (otherness) and freedom in terms analogous to objects and relations in physical space.[1] If transcendence is thought of in terms of physical spaciality, then, by definition, it must be opposed to immanence. For no body may occupy two locations simultaneously, and no location may be occupied simultaneously by two bodies. So if God is other and 'out there', God cannot be 'in here', and there must be an opposition between what comes from 'out there' and what comes from 'in here'; and consequently also an opposition between being oriented on what is 'in here' and on what is 'out there' and other. So even if we get as far as thinking that God might be magical enough to dwell 'in' me, God may only do so by displacing or squashing me. So if God and other people are other in this sense, whenever they move towards me in their own freedom, they are invading my space, my own being, with their alien being. And when I move towards them, then I either do so in my own freedom — in which case, I invade their space — or else I do so by abandoning my individual being and freedom in order to be domesticated in the order of their being and freedom. So being free in relation to what is other means invading others' space and/or protecting one's own.[2]

So, on this view, freedom is essentially a freedom *from*. A freedom from what is other in order to be oneself.[3] The personal centredness essential for autonomy, it is supposed, is a private place that has to be protected by fencing it off from the sphere of relation, and therefore from the otherness of God and one's

[1] In our common identification of this problem and our similar explorations of alternative means of conceptualization, both Colin Gunton and I are indebted to Daniel W. Hardy. See Colin E. Gunton's *The Promise of Trinitarian Theology* (Edinburgh: T&T Clark, 1991), pp.111ff., 117, 131-4; my own *The Call to Personhood: A Christian Theory of the Individual in Social Relationships* (Cambridge: Cambridge University Press, 1990), pp.79-86, 91, 100, 232f., and cf. with Hardy, 'Coleridge on the Trinity', *Anglican Theological Review,* LXIX (1988), 145-55.

[2] For Hobbes (in *Leviathan* [Oxford: Basil Blackwell, 1935], e.g. pp.82, 117), and for liberal contract theories of society generally, the free pursuit of private self-interest has this naturally conflicting form, since the otherness of individuals means that their interests must be opposed.

[3] Karl Barth not only sees the dispensability of God and neighbour as coincident, but considers the disorder of relation to God as the source of disorder in relation to neighbour. See *Church Dogmatics* IV/2 (Edinburgh: T&T Clark, 1958), pp.420f., 434f., 441ff. He characterizes this disorder in Kantian fashion as rejection of a universal law in favour of the universalization of one's own particular 'law'. See, e.g., *CD* IV/2, p.436. Similarly, the loss of properly ordered relationality with God and others leads to a breakdown in the conditions for proper subjectivity and individuality. See *CD* IV/1 (T&T Clark, 1956), pp.465f.

neighbours. Autonomy is then something one has in self-posses-sion, apart from relation to God or others, in an exclusive and private orientation on a supposedly asocial personal centre. So autonomy is principally construed as the private and individual self-determination of being, the potent form of which — especially in our consumer culture — is freedom of the will in choosing. Freedom and autonomy are had apart from relationship: they inhere within oneself. They are the basis on which one subse-quently enters relation.

On this account, since transcendence and immanence are bound to be opposed, human and divine freedom must in essence be competitive. If God has this kind of freedom, then divine sovereignty will have the appearance of tyranny. If we think of God as completely other, then we are obliged to define the sover-eign freedom that belongs to God as creator as alien, coercive power working from the outside: a power that invades our space and brooks no resistance. Consequently, the operation of divine power and freedom excludes any place for real creaturely free-dom.[4] Creatures then become objects for and of God's manipula-tion; in relation to God, they have to abandon all subjectivity and become passive recipients of the divine will.

If human beings have freedom of this kind, then they are condemned either to tyrannize or to be tyrannized by others; condemned to live without God and therefore without limit and without the dependencies and reciprocities of mutual enabling and assisting in being. On this interpretation, human freedom in relation to God may only be exercised by trying to do away with God and moving into the space which God once occupied.

---

[4] The possibilities of relating God to creation at all, and hence affirming the efficacy of the divine sovereignty — are actually undermined when God's transcendence and otherness are defined in extreme forms, since potent agency requires some form of connection — and therefore less than total differentiation. A 'wholly other' God would be impotent. The transcendence and otherness of God who is creator and redeemer is not served by collapsing these terms into easy notions of contrast which, paradoxically, bind God in terms of a negative definition in relation to the world — which is a relation of dependency on what the world is. Kathryn Tanner, *God and Creation in Christian Theology: Tyranny or Empowerment?* (Oxford: Basil Blackwell, 1988), pp.45ff., 56f., 78ff., 82, speaks of a non-contrastive transcendence. Cf. also Dietrich Bonhoeffer's criticism of the opposition of transcendence with immanence in *Letters and Papers from Prison* (London: SCM Press, 1971), pp.282, 311f., 336f., 341, 344f., 361, 381.

The misconstrual of sin as essentially pride

At this point, we may understand why the tradition's emphasis on the primacy of the sin of pride is problematic. Where pride is taken to be the primary and basic form of all sin,[5] then we are obliged to construe divine and human freedom as competitive, and equate any and all self-assertion as sinful. Pride is a sin, but it is not sin in its basic and root form, and its essence lies not in refusing to be nothing before God's tyrannical sovereignty, but in the refusal to stand in the order, economy and ecology of relation to God in which one may be something — but only in dependence on God. Naturally, such a view appears incoherent where dependence and freedom are understood to be simple opposites.

Insofar as pride denotes the attempt to be without God by turning oneself into a self-constituting, radically independent and sovereign subject, of worshipping oneself as absolute, then it certainly does constitute a sin. For one is not present in the order of a relationship to God — primarily in the supposition that one may only have one's freedom without or in opposition to God (and, indeed, to others). But if the essence of pride is actually a particular misdirection of worship — the identification of oneself as absolute or ultimate good — then it is best considered as a form of idolatry, which I hold to be the primary and root sin.[6] Pride is sin because it is a corruption of our relation to God: put simply, it is one form of distorted worship, and it is distorted worship that is the root of the distortions in our relationships to ourselves and to others. But pride, on this basis, need not be equated with any and all acts of self-assertion, self-protection or self-retrieval. Those acts may sometimes constitute the sin of pride, but they might at other times be positive requirements of right worship of God.

---

[5]   Barth, Niebuhr and Tillich all make this error. See: Barth, *CD* IV/1, pp.142, 358, 412-19, 421-3, 431f., 460, 464f., 745; Paul Tillich, *Systematic Theology* II (London: SCM Press, 1978), pp.47-50; Reinhold Niebuhr, *The Nature and Destiny of Man* I (London: Nisbet, 1941), pp.198-220.

[6]   The earliest extant Christian recognition of this is Tertullian, *De Idolatria* (Leiden: Brill, 1987), pp.24ff. In relation to our present theme, it is interesting to note that idolatry involves a mistake about transcendence. God's transcendence is either so stressed that relation to the world is threatened, or else the divine is located in some aspect of the world.

A conversation with feminism

The feminist discussion of sin and pride is illuminating here.[7] Its basic starting point is the situation and experience of many women of being in a systematically distorted network of relationships in which they are called to give themselves, to centre themselves in and orientate themselves towards others: to order themselves in an economy of relation determined by others' needs, which easily degenerates into vicious cycles of dependency and self-alienation. The consequence of this is a dissipation or loss of self, of having no self — either to assert or to deny. Thus some women in these situations find that they cease to be subjects for themselves, since they have ceased to be so for others, thereby experiencing a loss of freedom. If sin is pride, understood as any form of self-assertion or autonomy, then women have an obligation to stay in their situation of self-denial and self-giving.

Much feminist theology issues from a reinterpretation of this basic experience, which requires a reinterpretation of the tradition. Feminist reinterpretation is bound up in the process of women becoming subjects for themselves by naming the world and divine reality from the perspective given in their own experience; in particular, by naming self-loss, the failure to assert and honour oneself, the refusal of freedom and acquiescence in oppression as sin.[8] However, at this point, the analysis tends to be unhinged from

---

7   See Valerie Saiving, 'The Human Situation: A Feminine View', *Journal of Religion*, 40 (1960), 100-12; Susan Brooks Thistlethwaite, *Sex, Race and God: Christian Feminism in Black and White* (London: Chapman, 1990), ch. 5; Daphne Hampson, 'Luther on the Self: A Feminist Critique' in Ann Loades, ed., *Feminist Theology: A Reader* (London: SPCK, 1990), ch. 18; idem, *Theology and Feminism* (Oxford: Blackwell, 1990); Mary Daly, *Beyond God the Father: Towards a Philosophy of Women's Liberation* (London: The Women's Press, 1973), ch. 2; Mary Grey, *Redeeming the Dream: Feminism, Redemption and Christian Tradition* (London: SPCK, 1989), pp.15-19, 27, 91; Judith Plaskow, *Sex, Sin and Grace: Women's Experience and the Theologies of Reinhold Niebuhr and Paul Tillich* (Lanham, MD: UPA, 1980); Susan N. Dunfee, 'The Sin of Hiding: A Feminist Critique of Reinhold Niebuhr's Account of the Sin of Pride', *Soundings*, 65(3) (1982), 316-27; Wanda W. Berry, 'Images of Sin and Salvation in Feminist Theology', *Anglican Theological Review*, LX:I (1979), 25-54; Lucia Scherzberg, *Sünde und Gnade in der Feministischen Theologie* (Mainz: Grünewald, 1991).

8   Other feminist theologians operate with a more political perspective and tend, on the whole, to identify sin primarily in social, rather than psychological, terms. However, despite the emphasis on social structure, ideology and culture, rather than on the psychological dynamics of the individual self, these analyses also stress self-abnegation and

any specifically theological context, and hence from the dynamic of God's relation to us. The language of sin is retained, but without its basic grammatical rule of reference to God. It is inserted into the dynamic of self-making as described by, say, psychology, so that a theological 'boo-word' may be added to the chorus decrying what is judged to be pathological for the formation of personhood and subjectivity. By uprooting the language of sin from its theological context in this way, we are prevented from seeing why we should view self-loss as a sin, as a breakdown in the relation with God as well as a breakdown in the conditions of human selfhood and relation.

It is not only in feminist discussions of sin that reference to God is unconsciously elided (and there are, indeed, precious few sustained discussions of sin in recent theology apart from feminist ones). But there are, I think, particular factors shaping feminist theologies that make the relating of sin explicitly to God rather problematic, and which help to explain the absence of God from the picture. The general feminist starting point, which I have referred to above, might be described as a painful awareness of the empirical consequences of the language of dependence; and especially of evaluating oneself primarily in relation to what is other or transcendent, whether it be a human male or God. Self-loss, the opposite of pride, is to be objected to on account of what it does to women (and others); that is, with reference to the self and its intrinsic value and dynamic, rather than with reference to someone or something that transcends the self. Beneath the surface, I believe there is operating here an understandable suspicion that to speak of transcendence, especially together with talk of praise, can only be to speak of dependence in the form of domination.

As a very general observation, it might be said that feminists more usually tend to operate with a highly relational view of reality, including the self, an ontology that is not entirely consistent with the equation of transcendence with domination. It is not uncommon to find in feminist discussion an explicit rejection of the patriarchal way of being a self by asserting oneself over against

acquiescence in oppression as characteristic of the sin of women. Furthermore, reference to God in the description of sin is either absent or redundant here too. I would therefore tentatively suggest that the following criticisms might also apply to the use of the language of sin by some of those feminist theologians whose concern with the psychological is not dominant. (By way of example, see Rosemary R. Ruether, *Sexism and God-talk* [London: SCM Press, 1983], pp.113f., 160-4, 174, 180-3.)

others. Instead, there is an emphasis on relation with the otherness of other people, particularly in sisterly community, which might be conceived of as being constituted by a circulation of praise. This vision of relation and community is founded on the transcendence or otherness of the participants, as one is empowered through the proximity of others in a community of interdependence. There is, naturally, a very live awareness of the ambiguities of speaking in relational terms, and of the consequent dangers of such talk being (deliberately?) misconstrued, so that it is turned again into a justification for dependence and domination (of weak, relational selves [stereotypically women] by strong, unrelated ones [stereotypically men] — which explains why some feminists exclude men from membership of the community). But the force of the feminist insight that right relation does not imply self-alienation is such that the language of relation is maintained, despite the dangers of its meaning being misconstrued if it is translated into a patriarchal framework.

When it comes to God, however, the reservations concerning the language of transcendence and relation are usually more acute. I think that this may be due to the fear of any relation that appears to be hierarchical and therefore enslaving. In relation to the transcendent God, there is an inevitable asymmetry, such that is not inevitable in interpersonal relations. The relation is ordered in a way that secures the precedence of one partner in relation to another. And feminists often here adopt the liberal reaction to that kind of talk, interpreting this order as a threat to human autonomy, thinking that it can and must imply that here women are confronted by another patriarchal male. Here there is a tendency to slip back into patriarchal notions (usually in liberal form) that relation is a threat to one's being, a resistance to the idea that the self and its freedom might be given through relation; more specifically, in relations of an asymmetrical form. God's transcendence appears to be a problem from a feminist standpoint.

Feminist theology has invested a good deal of energy in the reinterpretation of God. Significantly, the problem driving feminist reconstructions of the understanding of God has been precisely this question of transcendence or otherness over against immanence or proximity. The reconceptions that, in my view, are most problematic are those which go for immanence as if it were a simple opposite of transcendence, as it has been understood in patriarchal conceptions. That seems to me to be both inadequate to the transcendence of the Christian God and to be tied still to a dichotomous way of thinking, which is often dubbed as patriarchal. Those reconceptions which seem to me to do most justice to the trinitarian being of God (even when not explicitly trinitarian) and genuinely to move beyond the patriarchal are those which attempt to unite otherness with proximity, transcendence with immanence, in some way.[9]

If God's otherness and transcendence are of a patriarchal kind, then we are left with the overemphasis on the sin of pride that the feminist discussion rightly finds so problematic, as well as a misconstrual of pride as any form of self-assertion. For such a god may only jealously guard the space which is rightly his; and such a god does not make space for others. If, on the other hand, one operates with a view of God as so immanent as to be indistinguishable from the biological or social processes which foster selfhood and subjectivity, then explicit mention of God is redundant, since it adds nothing more than a rhetorical flourish to the characterization of those processes to say that God is active within them, or to relate their distortion to God by naming it as sin. Were these the only alternatives, then one would either have to give up on transcendence or on God altogether. It is perhaps significant that this is how a number of feminist theologians see the choice.

Is it too simplistic to suggest that the feminist discussion of the sin of pride fails to be theological for two connected reasons? First, the problem that is identified and which sets the agenda is the adequacy of an emphasis on the sin of pride to fit the experience and situation of women, without reference to God (is this equivalent to saying that the situation of women is more important and urgent than that of God?). Pride (interpreted as having too much self), it is accepted, is problematic, but it is spoken of as such only in relation to other human selves. Consequently, self-loss is also interpreted only as an interpersonal and personal evil. It distorts the proper dynamic of being a self. Second, can it be that the participants in this discussion of sin operate with simple models of transcendence and immanence, such as those above, and therefore believe themselves faced with a stark choice between transcendence and immanence? If that is the case, then it would provide a positive reason for the exclusion of God from the discussion of sin, since the transcendent God cannot be brought close to human selves without disempowering and dominating them; whilst the immanent God is so identified with the processes of selfhood that there is no reason to make that presence explicit. Indeed, it would look like a needless complication to relate the sins of selfhood to the language of God. If there is something in this

9   Such as Sallie McFague's Mother, Lover, Friend (see her *Metaphorical Theology* [London: SCM Press, 1982] and *Models of God: Theology for an Ecological, Nuclear Age* [London: SCM Press, 1987]). Whatever criticisms may be levelled against these images for God, they are attempts to understand the transcendence of God as enabling rather than disabling of human being.

hunch, then the absence of God from the discussion may be partly due to the perceived unavailability of models of God as transcendent, yet empowering and enabling of human selfhood.

Were such models to operate in the feminist discussion of sin, then there might be reason to affirm that self-loss is indeed a sin, and in essence the same sin as the sin of pride.[10] If, instead of asking what total devotion to, dependence on and loss of the self in another are in relation to the self and its freedom, we ask what they are in relation to God, we can see the sin immediately for what it is: idolatry. And the cure for idolatry is conversion of the self (or society or group or institution) to right worship. The question posed to us by the concerns of feminist theologians is whether we can arrive at a conception of God that does not make the cure worse than the disease. Is the setting aside of the self for God really any different from the abrogation of freedom and subjectivity involved in self-loss?

III. The Triune God who Loves in Freedom

Despite its best insights, then, the feminist discussion of the sin of pride appears to have an unreformed understanding of God's sovereignty and of human autonomy operationally underlying it. Insofar as this account is accurate, feminist theology appears to be repeating the same set of assumptions that have led to the problematic interpretation and emphasis on pride. Perhaps it is a little oversimplistic, although not without its truth, to say: both the tradition and feminist theology have constructed an idol. The tradition has done so in order to resist claims made for human freedom; feminists, to resist claims made for God's freedom. For in both, God is posited as precisely the kind of subject that, in *hubris*, the human tries to be. Consequently, both carry the assumption that the corollary of God's sovereignty is human insignificance.[11]

---

[10] Feminist theologians might begin here by extending the suggestive analysis of patriarchy as idolatry. That insight underlies almost all of feminist theology, especially in its recasting of language, even where it is not explicitly thematized or articulated. See especially the work of Sallie McFague.

[11] Compare again the position of Kathryn Tanner, who suggests that modern conceptions of freedom in terms of the power of free self-determination when applied to God produce a tyrant; when applied to humankind, move in a radically Pelagian direction virtually negating the need for divine agency. That both emphases may occur together explains why Christian discourse tends to become incoherent in the modern period. See *God and Creation*, pp.121ff., 152f., 157-60. Cf. again with Bonhoeffer, *Letters and Papers*, pp.311, 326, 381.

But since this is not an adequate characterization of the Christian God, this is the making of an idol.

For the living God of the Christian story is not this kind of isolated, absolute monarch, but One who is constituted by a radical form of relation, mutuality and reciprocity in which freedom is given to what is other. Thus the tradition finds itself having to speak of God as a tri-unity of Persons, and is obliged by God's history of self-giving freedom to define God's being as love. Face to face with the God of Jesus Christ, we are liberated from this awful dichotomy, that we must either live solely out of our own freedom, power and resources or solely out of God's — in which case, there is no place for human freedom and responsibility. It is only through the triune God's being and relation to the world that we know what it means to speak of sin as a refusal of or assault on God's sovereignty and freedom. The triune identity of the God who loves in freedom requires a radicalization of terms such as sovereignty, lordship and freedom that modifies the effect of the proper insistence that sin be related to God's sovereign freedom.

The incarnation: space for humanity and God?

We can see immediately that orthodox faith in Christ requires us to think of transcendence and immanence, of God and humanity, together.[12] To proclaim a form of identification between God and the crucified Jesus also immediately suggests that God's freedom and sovereignty are of a radically different kind from the way we ordinarily take them to be. Incarnation in the body of the crucified one implies that God's freedom does not, after all, entail a transcendent aloofness from the world, but a form of involvement with it in which the divine being and freedom are staked. God subjects Godself to the risks, vulnerabilities and ambiguities of historical existence, including the risk of rejection, suffering and death, as

---

[12] That is not to say that the conceptual difficulties of so doing do not exist or can be ignored. They cannot. But that is a far cry from saying that we must first consider these conceptual difficulties in the abstract, and only then and on that basis see what we may say about God and humanity in Christ. Rather, we must first see what we are obliged to say about God and humanity when we see them in Christ, and only then and on that basis consider the rationality of our talk. It will be of particular importance to avoid the illusion that we may find some conceptually neat solution without losing the essence of Christian faith. Orthodox Christianity requires the maintenance of conceptual ambiguities and paradox.

well as of misinterpretation. God's freedom and sovereignty must be of a radical kind: the freedom to give oneself in relation; to be with and in creation in ways which are costly to God, but which do not abrogate God's sovereignty, freedom and transcendence.[13]

But this also has implications for human freedom in relation to God. For here we see God communicating and relating, not as a tyrannical, absolute sovereign, but in and through the form of a human person; indeed, by uniting the divine freedom of self-giving with that of a human person. So God's countermove to the misuse of human freedom in sin is not to coerce compliance, nor to overrule the rejection and the freedom that issued it, nor yet to squash the rebellion with majestic, divine power. Neither does God do nothing and merely accept the new state of affairs. We may have willed to be without God, but God does not will to be God without us.[14] God does something infinitely more creative than either giving up on us or coercing us into compliance. We are not left to our own devices. But instead of brute force, which may be characterised as the manipulation of objects, we are confronted by God in the form of another human person. That is to say that, in the Christ-event, we are confronted by a divine power that is radically personal, and which consequently effects itself through forms of interpersonal communication and personal presence that make creative appeal to human freedom.[15] So this is not monologue, but a dialogue in which we are intended and respected as subjects. Its primary form is the unity between God and Jesus, where the free movement of God to and for humanity receives appropriate response in the free, yet obedient, movement of a human person towards and for God.[16]

---

[13] So Barth, *CD*, IV/1, pp.417f., 466f.

[14] For Barth, this decision of God's, whilst not overpowering, is nonetheless determinative of 'reality' and, for this reason, sin must be considered a non-real reality over against the divine decision-in-action. For a clear example, see *CD* IV/2, pp.408-11. Hence God may be said to be free in relation to sin.

[15] Cf. Barth at *CD* I/2, p.661. On the importance and utility in this respect of maintaining personal language for God, see Tanner, *God and Creation*, pp.69, 72f., 102f.; D. W. Hardy & D. F. Ford, *Jubilate: Theology in Praise* (London: Darton, Longman & Todd, 1984) pp.79ff.

[16] This is evidenced in both the form and content of Jesus' ministry and proclamation. He proclaims the good news of God's forgiveness and the proximity of the kingdom, which is experienced as liberation for God and, as a direct consequence, for others and — on that basis — for oneself; he does so in dialogical manner which intends and seeks the integrity and autonomy of the other in making response (particularly in the use of parables, which allow the audience interpretive freedom in provoking insight, rather than coercing or imposing a view).

It is not inaccurate, but it is insufficient, merely to say that, in Christ we find the divine power manifest in weakness. It is more that here we find God subjecting Godself, first of all to the limitation of incarnation in a human person; secondly, allowing Godself to be subject to human freedom — even to the extent of death — to bear the consequences of the human refusal of freedom on Godself. And yet the crucifixion is similarly not permitted to become the last word and final reality. The sin of humanity in crucifying God is creatively reworked by God into the event in which the very power of sin and death are themselves overcome. Again, this does not happen by disallowing that death, but by making it the occasion for a proleptic anticipation of the total victory of life over death and of freedom over the power of sin, wickedness and evil. And that victory does not come, in the end, through the exercise of divine power in a way that excludes free human agency. It comes in a way that radically includes it — in the first instance, by uniting Godself with a human person in and through whose free obedience the drama of God with us unfolds. God will not have this victory over our heads, but only through our engagement in active responsibility towards this future that is set before us, and so God suffers our refusal of this future. The resurrection is not, then, the belated cancellation of the possibilities of human freedom through the undoing of that which it has achieved, by returning Jesus to life. It is, rather, simultaneously the refusal to allow communication to be closed down[17] and the empowering and resourcing of the possibilities of human freedom — not as the freedom to be without God (although this remains an empirical possibility), but as the freedom to be with and for God in a way that appropriately responds to God's being with and for us. A notion of freedom adequate to this fact cannot, then, be the freedom to be contrary to or to withdraw from God. It is, instead, a relational form of freedom: primarily to be construed in terms of the call to conform to Christ.[18] This is a call into active responsibility in the form of discipleship: a free following into the open future with God in community.

[17] Cf. Hardy & Ford, *Jubilate*, p.126, who speak of the resurrection as a referral of Jesus back to the world. (On the logic of crucifixion, see also pp.79f.)

[18] Cf. my development of this theme in *The Call to Personhood*, esp. ch. 2. The fact that this takes the form of following a person, rather than the assent to eternal truths, has implications for the nature and communication of Christian truth, which I tentatively explore in 'Truth as Mission: The Christian Claim to Universal Truth in a Pluralist Public World', *Scottish Journal of Theology*, 46 (1993), 437-56.

And so we find that an understanding of transcendence modelled on an analogy with physical space, together with the correlative interpretation of freedom, is inadequate to express the freedom and sovereignty of God with humanity which is revealed in the incarnation and crucifixion. In particular, we find that the incarnation compels us to find ways of speaking of divine and human freedom as correlated — asymmetrically so, but correlated nonetheless. In respect of the divine-human union in Christ, orthodoxy has always found it necessary to employ metaphorical or paradoxical language in order to speak of the unity between God and humanity in Christ. The permanent intention of orthodoxy in its deployment of language has been to affirm that divinity and humanity are together in their integrity. Neither the divine sovereignty nor the dignity and freedom of humanity are reduced by being joined together. On God's side, there is no giving up of transcendence in this proximity to humanity, or of sovereign freedom in this limitation. God does not cease to be God; in Christ, God really encounters us as God. Furthermore, the affirmation of divine transcendence cannot only apply to the Father. That would be a reversion to an understanding of transcendence, modelled on the analogue of physical space, which keeps the Father distantly aloof. It would also involve a reneging on the commitment to maintain the Son's transcendence whilst incarnate. So our position is reinforced, that orthodox Christian faith requires different notions of transcendence that, in this instance, preserve the Son's transcendence even whilst radically immanent. If transcendence and presence are to be construed in ways analogous to physical space, then God cannot become present without giving up transcendence, and God and humanity cannot be located simultaneously in the same physical body: if God invades the space of a human being with sovereignty intact, that can only mean the suppression or evacuation of the human in a kind of human *kenosis*. And hence we would be forced to give up the central affirmation of Christian faith.

In order to speak of the God who is for us in Christ, we need to adopt social conceptions of space and personal notions of presence and of unity, rather than brute physical ones.[19]

---

[19] Cf. Bonhoeffer's notion of ethical transcendence introduced in *Sanctorum Communio: A Dogmatic Enquiry into the Sociology of the Church* (London: Collins, 1963), pp.29, 31-4. This understanding of space and presence is also necessary in the doctrine of the Trinity, and occurs at least implicitly in those major streams of the tradition which speak of the union between the trinitarian Persons and between the Son and Jesus in terms of willing and action (Augustine and the

Divine and human freedom in creation and redemption: dialogue

I have been arguing that, on the human side, incarnation does not involve a humiliation, but an exaltation of humanity; not an invasion of our space, but an invitation into freedom. For in Christ, God is present in an orientation towards and radically for us all. And in that being for us and movement towards us, we are taken seriously in our integrity and freedom and called freely to participate, to move ourselves and become followers of God in Christ, in response to God's movement towards us.

Since, however, this movement of God towards us does involve an opposition to what we empirically and presently are in the state of sin, and since redemption requires a reorientation in obedience to God in which we leave our present selves behind, the question once again arises as to whether this is not simple heteronomy. Can we make good the claim that obedience to this call, in which we conform ourselves to Christ, is not merely made *in* freedom (in which case, freedom might only exist at this point of decision, as a freedom to choose the unfreedom of obedience), but that it actually *is* freedom itself? Can we show that what is realized in Christ is our true humanity and not something alien? To do so requires us to show some continuity between creation and redemption. Such continuity is to be expected, not only on account of the monotheistic affirmation that the agent of both creation and redemption is the same; it is required also by a trinitarianism that affirms that the Word incarnate in Christ and active with the Spirit in redemption is also an active agent in the trinitarian economy of creation.

Creation clearly has to relate to God's freedom — it is a free act of God's sovereignty. It is contingent on nothing other than God's being and freedom. However, if we take the doctrine of the Trinity seriously, we also have to say that this freedom is inadequately conceived of as an unforced and non-contingent act, if that implies that it is simply arbitrary. God's inmost being is constituted by the radical mutuality of the three divine Persons, in which they both give and receive their individuality from one another. In their intersubjectivity, there is the creative intention and recognition of subjectivity, and therefore of transcendence in the form of the integrity of personal identity, in the giving of space to one another. This giving of space is an interpersonal event, and must not be thought of as analogous to the evacuation of physical

Western traditions rooted in him), as well as in those branches of the tradition which speak of the trinitarian unity in terms of community (e.g., the Cappadocians).

space. It is not a form of absence, but a way of being present with others in creative recognition of their autonomy *within the relationship*. It is a letting-be, rather than a letting-go: a structuring of the relation so that it includes space and time for personal discreteness and autonomous response.[20] Thus the trinitarian life involves a circulation of the divine potentialities of being through the processes of self-giving, in the unity of which the three Persons receive their distinct personal identities. What is truly personal and inexchangeable arises in and through this relation, where the orientation of one on another is so intense that we must again defeat the analogy with physical spatiality and speak of the mutual indwelling of identities (*perichoresis*).

The joy and freedom of this mutuality of love is so creative and full of overflowing potentiality that, in a sense, it would fail to find satisfaction if locked up in itself.[21] And so creation is not simply an expression or externalization of the divine love; creation is caught up in, both sustained in being and redeemed by, the trinitarian life of love — primarily through the personal presence and activity of the Son and Spirit. And if creation is caught up in the divine reciprocity of the giving and receiving of being, it means that we are unable to think of God's transcendence in terms of spatial distance, since the transcendence of the trinitarian creator also includes personal presence and indwelling in history (not confined to the human, but including all of creation). It must also include a form of transcendence that is more analogous to the personal, and which does not exclude God's proximity as and at the very centre of our being.[22]

---

[20] This is all rather sketchy and schematic. For a fuller presentation, see *The Call to Personhood* (on personal transcendence and the giving of space, pp.32ff., 42f., 60ff., 126-9, 133-8; on this view of subjectivity and autonomy, pp.32f., 70f., 76f., 81f., 147f., 228f., 263ff.).

[21] It is impossible to avoid language which carries some implication of unwilled emanation — but if the overspilling is of love, then we should be able to avoid the implication that this excludes the divine freedom. The point is that God's subjectivity has the form of intersubjectivity already in God's inmost being. The love which we encounter in God's freedom towards us (in Barthian terms, God's Act) is not an arbitrary whim. So in God's relation to us we do encounter the real God as God is in Godself, not just as God is for us. It is more important, in my judgement to defeat any implication of arbitrariness, occasionalism or modalism than it is to protect oneself from all possibilities of misunderstanding that creation might be an unintentional act.

[22] See Bonhoeffer's position at *The Cost of Discipleship* (London: SCM Press, 1959), p.65 and *Creation and Fall: A Theological Interpretation of Genesis 1-3* (London: SCM Press, 1959) p.52 and *Letters and Papers*, pp.282, 387.

One immediate consequence of this way of speaking is a dynamic, relational conception of what it means for humanity to image God. For if God is not a static being 'out there', but a community of persons in movement towards and present in creation, opening up a new future of freedom, then imaging God must correspondingly be a dynamic affair.[23] It also restrains us from speaking of a simple dichotomy between obedience to a God 'out there' and human autonomy, or of the autonomy of creation more generally, since God is not only 'out there' but free to work 'in here' too.[24] And if the 'in here' is already ordered and structured 'naturally' by the presence and activity of God, we have further reason to suspect that the language of heteronomy does us a disservice.

We have come to a point where we can begin to see that the creative and redemptive work of the triune God requires us to speak of divine presence and activity, not as space invasion, but as the creative giving of space; and of sovereignty and freedom as freedom to take seriously the autonomy-in-relation of creation. As I have already suggested, this does not mean leaving us alone and letting us 'go to the devil'. What we have to do with here is a form of presence in which even the negative consequences of creaturely freedom are taken seriously.[25] God takes them on Godself in order

---

[23] Cf. Wolfhart Pannenberg, *Theology and the Kingdom of God* (Philadelphia: Westminster Press, 1969), pp.70f., for whom the eschatological nature of the doctrine of creation is necessary to secure human autonomy as a movement of (self-) transcendence from the dead past into the freedom of the future. The eschatological future becomes, for him, a necessary correlate of both divine and human freedom. That is, in my view, an unnecessary overstatement which leads his theology into a number of difficulties, not least that the focus effectively moves from the triune intersubjectivity in which God has being to an operationally formal understanding of the future.

[24] This seems to be implied by the language of transformation when applied to redemption, since that carries the implication of radical change alongside some form of continuity with the past. Further, if sin is a total corruption of our spirit (our way of being in the world in relation to God, others and oneself), then we are incapable of righting the situation ourselves. Redemption must therefore come from an external agency, but must work on us from within as well as without. Hence, where the tradition emphasizes the conversion of human inwardness, there is a recognition that human autonomy *is* engaged. But, since God is redemptively present even at the core of individual subjectivity, we are not without God even in our free acceptance of what comes to us in and as grace.

[25] Cf. Hardy & Ford, *Jubilate*, p.81.

to ensure that the future is not entirely lost to them,[26] but may engage with and transform the world, and may do so precisely at the point of its distortion and brokenness. This happens, then, through a transformation of the world as it has become through and in sin by means that engage the freedom and sinfulness of the creature in the processes of transformation: faith, hope and love.

In respect of the doctrine of creation, then, this would imply that we have to do here with both God's transcendent sovereignty as creator and human autonomy: transcendence of a personal, and autonomy of a relational, kind. We must find a way of speaking of autonomy, then, which relates it to the freedom of God[27] creatively to intend creaturely autonomy in communication: the freedom to give space for that which may only exist on the basis of this giving. We must speak, then, of our autonomy as a gift of God,[28] so that our freedom depends on God's freedom in relation with us. The polarity of freedom and dependence is consequently a further supposed opposition that is undermined in the logic of the position I am unfolding.

The consciousness of the Old Testament is permeated by precisely this double-aspect of being in relation to God: depend-

[26] Because the future of salvation is secured by God in this way, we may say that God remains free in relation to sin. For Barth's understanding of this, see *CD*, IV/2, p.410.

[27] God's communication is free, since (a) it is not bound to respect something which was already in existence independently, but respects that which is and can only stand independently over against God on account of God's free willing; (b) it is undeserved by any merit on the part of the recipients; (c) it affords free space for response, and therefore also includes the possibilities of misunderstanding, rejection, disobedience and disbelief; and (d) is willing to take up the consequences of human freedom but is not bound by the possibilities inherent in them.

[28] This conforms to Tanner's rule that, 'Non-divine being must be talked about as always and in every respect constituted by, and therefore nothing apart from, an immediate relation with the founding agency of God' (*God and Creation*, p.84). She is clear that this not only does not negate the possibility of free creaturely agency (pp.88ff.), but enables divine agency in its freedom to work through sufficient created causes — thus freeing God from the compulsion to work through coercive, irresistible power (p.159f.). Thus the dependence of creaturely freedom on God turns out to be a means of securing its integrity. I know from my students just how powerful is the individualistic resistance in our culture to the language of gift, especially in the interpersonal sphere. The automatic assumption is that giving must put the recipient in a relationship of self-alienating dependency. And so the language of gift is often met with the resistance of the language of rights, specifically rights to self-assertion and determination.

ence on the sovereignty and initiative of God in creation and human history, especially Israel's election, together with freedom in response. In the Old Testament, it is constantly reinforced that election and covenant were dependent on the free gift of God, not on any merit in Israel. So the basis of salvation, whatever else might be demanded, was not Israel's choice of, or freedom to choose, God; it was God's choice of Israel. Everything else followed from the free, joyful and grateful acceptance of that understanding of Israel's basic situation before God.[29] And here is our main clue: the counterpart to dependence on God's freedom in giving us space for freedom-in-response is the celebration of that gift in its return through grateful acceptance. Our freedom before God does not therefore consist primarily in our *arbitrium* in which we may reject God, but in our *voluntas*, wherein we might make appropriate free response. So the autonomy we are given is a form of freedom, but it is freedom with intent: that we might realize the freedom in making appropriate response to God. A necessary corollary of being set at a distance from God so that we might make free response is that we also have the freedom not to respond aright — so our freedom to be contrary is something like an epiphenomenon of our being posited by God as free to respond aright.[30]

Israel's election was therefore both blessing and special responsibility. The self-giving of God to Israel is in the first place an indicative: 'I am your God, I belong to you', in which there is the dual assurance of the divine presence and of being set in free space over against God as recipients of the divine choosing for partnership. And only subsequently, on that amazing basis, is it an imperative:[31] 'obey my word, keep the commandments' (Ex 19-20). Since the imperative rests on the indicative of God's self-giving love in which God elects to be for and with Israel, it is liberative and free. What is entailed is the free and grateful acceptance of what it means to be the people of God, to respond to and actualize

---

[29] This is a major theme in Deuteronomy. See, for example, 4.32-40, 7.6-11, 9.4-6, 10.16f., 23.5. Cf. here Barth's understanding of autonomy at *CD*, II/2, pp.176f.

[30] The notion of being created at an 'epistemic distance' from God in order to safeguard freedom is a crucial aspect of John Hick's theodicy, which bears some analogical correspondence with what I suggest here, despite the very real differences in our central positions. See his *Evil and the God of Love* (Glasgow: Fount, 1979), pp.316-27.

[31] Cf. Emil Brunner's comments in relation to creation at *Man in Revolt* (London: Lutterworth, 1939), pp.98, 104f.

the fact of being chosen by God by freely choosing God.[32] The commandments underscore what it means in terms of responsible human agency and to turn towards the divine love into the free space of the future. God's free love is not dependent on appropriate human response, but it does actively seek it,[33] in terms of both belief and action.

Responsibility requires autonomy.[34] In respect of creation and redemption, we also have to say that this autonomy does not have its foundation in some unrelated, independent aspect of our humanity (and much less our individuality). Rather, it is founded upon the divine call to make autonomous response to God. Its foundation is not in our separation, but precisely in this form of relation in which God posits, wills and then calls us to have the otherness, independence, transcendence and autonomy of a community of persons in relation: in the giving of space in which we may have the freedom of creatures before the self-giving of God. Our freedom is to respond to God by entering into dialogue partnership. And since our freedom has its basis in relation to God's movement towards us — in which God is with and for us in personal form, and therefore posits and wills us to bear the freedom of persons — if we posit ourselves apart from this relation, we forfeit our freedom. Freedom must then approximate to our freedom for God; our freedom to respond to God's free movement towards us. And the implication cannot be avoided here that this relational form of autonomy — of being a subject in and through relation — is actually intensified in its proximity to God's sovereign freedom: not diminished, but intensified in the circulation of God's creative letting-be and human praise of God.

32 So Barth, *CD*, IV/1, pp.423f., 430. This also appears to be the basic understanding of D. A. Carson, *Divine Sovereignty and Human Responsibility: Biblical Perspectives in Tension* (Atlanta: John Knox, 1981), p.21.
33 Carson makes such an observation in his examination of Johannine soteriology, citing John 14.21, 16.27 in *Divine Sovereignty*, p.197.
34 The language of responsibility remains here a theological language, since it may only be understood in the context of our being called by God. We ought, then, to resist its being illegitimately uprooted from its reference to God as the caller before whom we are responsible for our answers. Because of the retention of the reference to God in its use in this context, we may correspondingly speak of irresponsibility as sin — as the 'violation of a personal bond'. The term is Paul Ricoeur's, see *The Symbolism of Evil* (Boston: Beacon, 1969), p.52.

IV. Praise and the Image

This autonomy is appropriately and fully realized primarily and paradigmatically in the freedom of praise and thanksgiving.[35] Praise is the free response to God's free grace; the appropriate response to what comes as gift rather than demand.[36] Gift elicits freedom on the part of the recipient, it does not impose itself primarily in the character of obligation, duty, work; rather, it excites the unforced play of freedom in praise.

In the Old Testament, we find Israel's emerging consciousness that their relationship with God is personal in the sense that, in it, a free response in thanks and praise is expected, intended and enabled (being understood to include responsible action and relation in the horizontal plane as well as the vertical). The election of Israel may be construed as an invitation into dialogue-partnership with God. God addresses Israel as Thou, expecting them to be I's (i.e., communicatively autonomous) in response.[37] In the creation narratives, we find acknowledgement that Israel's special relationship with God is an intensification of the situation of all humanity before God. For all human beings are created for this dialogue partnership. Reading the creation narratives in a trinitarian light, we might say that humankind is intended to image the dynamic being and activity of God in love. We do so by returning the gift, by meeting God's movement towards us with the counterpoint of our movement towards God in thanksgiving and praise.[38] We do this by standing in the free space given to us, celebrating what has been given, affirming what we are in the limitation and humility of our creatureliness, but also in the seriousness with which God takes us as dialogue-partners and determination not to be without us. We do it by expanding into the space created by a God for us and with us in this manner, but doing so in the ordered ecology of a relation respectful of the divine sovereignty in the gift of grace, wherein we are given our freedom. Letting God be God, sovereign and Lord of all, in our willing, thinking and acting is the creaturely correspondence to God's letting us be, the giving of distance and freedom in relation. In

---

[35] In the Old Testament, the understanding that the appropriate response to God's sovereignty in creation and redemption has the mode of gratitude in praise is most clearly found in the Psalms. See, for example, Pss 24, 33, 104, 136, 148.

[36] Brunner, *Man in Revolt*, p.104.

[37] Cf. Barth, *CD*, III/1, pp.182ff.; Brunner, *Man in Revolt*, p.102.

[38] Barth designates human being as a being-in-gratitude at *CD*, III/2, p.166.

praise, we affirm that we only have our freedom from and in relation to God, and that God — simply as God — has a right to that freedom too. The freedom of praise is not withdrawal from, but intensification and celebration of, the relation: and through the celebration of God's freedom for us that we image in our freedom for God, our own being, freedom and possibilities for action become enhanced and intensified. In response to the space that we are given by God, we make and give space to God, and in that space find and know ourselves as in partnership with God in all our being, acting and thinking.[39] And this is not humiliation. It is more like being caught up in a movement of (mutual) wonder, surprise, joy and delight in the other — especially the other's freedom and particularity — and hence their very otherness.

And this praise of God is simultaneously an exaltation of humanity, since it reiterates the significance human being achieves in our designation as God's dialogue-partners in God's movement towards us. Paradigmatically, this occurs in the glorification of humanity in Christ, who is the archetype and prototype of this human imaging of God in the humble obedience in which we find ourselves liberated to be for God as God is for us. It celebrates God in a celebration of our human designation as God's dialogue partners. It is also freedom, since it signals our active entrance into the history of God for and with us.[40]

---

[39] Hence this is not an evacuation of ourselves from specially sanctified space onto which nobody dare tread. It is an orientation towards God, a finding of God with and for us in our own free space, which remains our own sphere of action even whilst we acknowledge that in it our autonomy is bound up with the sovereign freedom of God. At this point, we may begin to discern the necessity of affirming that free, faithful obedience involves God's as well as our own agency and may be described as a form of co-subjectivity. On this, see Barth, *Church Dogmatics*, for example, IV/1, pp.742f., IV/3 (T&T Clark, 1961), p.63; IV/4 (T&T Clark, 1969), pp.5f., 35, 41, 106, 141-4 (this theme is illuminated by George Hunsinger in *How to Read Karl Barth: The Shape of his Theology* [New York: Oxford University Press, 1991], ch. 7, as well as by John Macken in *The Autonomy Theme in the Church Dogmatics: Karl Barth and his Critics* [Cambridge: Cambridge University Press, 1990], passim); Carson, *Divine Sovereignty*, pp.36f., 210ff.; and Tanner's discussion in *God and Creation*, pp.56f., 92ff., 101f.

[40] Cf. again Barth's understanding of obedience, autonomy, heteronomy and theonomy, for example, *CD*, I/2, pp.857-61, IV/1, p.467 and also of subjectivity: III/2, pp.192, 194-7. See also the useful discussion of Macken in *The Autonomy Theme*, pp.31ff.

V. What, then, is Sin?

What, then, is sin in relation to all this? Sin is the denial of God, the refusal or blocking of proper praise. But since, as we have seen, God's being, sovereignty and transcendence are not static, but dynamic and radically relational in movement towards us, we must avoid thinking of either praise or sin in static terms. They have instead to be related to the dynamic freedom of God's being and action. Right praise is not basing oneself on a foundational and permanent, static equilibrium through the mediation of the past in the form of, say, creation, covenant, or even Christ (in the form of an already co-ordinated human response to God). All of these things are, indeed, mediations of God, but of God moving towards us and calling us to move towards the future with God. If we turn them, and hence God also, into some already achieved equilibrium in our relationship with God, then we are idolaters once again. Praise and sin have therefore to refer to a dynamic relation to God in which we are called into responsible activity in the world towards the future (discipleship). Active human response to God is the only image of God in the world. Any other image is an idol.

In view of the trinitarian nature of the God who loves in freedom, we can now say more precisely that sin is opposition to, an assault on, God's freedom. Opposing God's sovereignty and freedom, furthermore, entails opposition to our own being and freedom, as well as our future in salvation. Primarily and paradigmatically, sin has the form of idolatry: worshipping something other than the triune God who moves towards us in freedom, either by constructing false images of God or else by being oriented towards something in the world as if it were God. Sin is thus displacement and disengagement from the movement of God towards us by finding ourselves unable and unwilling to move towards, to image, God in response. In respect of the movement of God's freedom, sin is immobility.[41] It is a misconception therefore to call the orientation of corrupted praise freedom, since it connotes our inability to move towards and respond to the transcendent reality of God and others.

This assault on God's freedom may happen just as easily through a passive loss of self as through vital self-actualization. A condition of praise is not merely that one must have a self in order to give it freely to God — though that is, indeed, a necessary condition it is not sufficient by itself. For praise becomes impossible if the further condition is not met, that one believes oneself to be forgiven, affirmed, upheld, given, worth something — precisely

---

[41] So Barth, *CD*, IV/2, pp.383, 433, 452.

in the integrity and particularity of one's being — so that one both
has something to offer and something to be thankful for, some
reason to offer it. The denial of that, even within the pain and
brokenness of our lives, is ultimately an abandonment of faith and
hope. It is simultaneously abandonment of the God who creatively
and powerfully is loving the world back to freedom, and finds no
one and nothing in it unusable in the cause of their own freedom
— no matter how broken or apparently hopeless they may seem to
themselves or others.

So right praise of the true God is not a diminution or loss of
self; on the contrary, self-loss is a disruption of praise, since it is
a requirement of worship that one takes as seriously as God does
the freedom and integrity of one's own being. In praise, we affirm
God's act of giving space for us to be, in our integrity and
particularity. And because in praise we are precisely standing on
the ground of the particularity, integrity and freedom of our being
which God graciously grants us, in praise there is an intensification of our particularity, our integrity and of our freedom. In being
free for, with and in the One who loves us in freedom and seeks us
as dialogue-partners, we find our freedom in the particular economy
of relation to the triune God. And even where this might involve
conversion, a discovery that God's call opposes our present, empirical being, this is a conversion to our own true selves and to our
freedom. In conversion, we find that we are not de-centred but re-
centred,[42] and we also find that God is with us after all in the very
centre of our being — precisely at that point where we are most
particularly ourselves.

When we find ourselves unable to affirm our integrity and
particularity, then our praise is distorted, since we are incapable of
allowing our particularity and integrity to overflow. It is just as
distorted when we try to hold our integrity and particularity apart
from God (and others), as if they existed apart from the particular
order and economy of relation to God and others, as if they constituted private space which we may turn into self-referring praise.

---

[42] This is a conversion of our spirit, which regulates our being-in-relation
and personal identity. It is therefore worked from within and cannot
be construed in terms either of heteronomy or of self-alienation (since
it is a conversion away from present self-distortion). What is denoted
here, then, is not a lack of self, but a reorientation such that one is
centred, but is so in and through right relation to God (and so to others
too). See *The Call to Personhood* for a discussion of personal spirit as
the energy through which a person organizes communication, relation,
and hence the boundary between self and others (pp.55f., 63, 115f.,
151, 152-6, 252-5), and of ex-centric forms of centredness (pp.40, 57f.,
60, 126, 149, 151f., 156f.).

VI. Concluding Remarks

Since sin represents a loss of our freedom, then we may return to the premiss with which I began. With sin we have primarily to do with God's freedom, not ours. The mainstream Christian line has always maintained that freedom is what we lose in sin: not the freedom of the will as a capacity arbitrarily to choose, but the freedom to move and be moved in the direction of our own good.[43]

 What is lost in sin is our freedom to move towards the eschatological future with God, and therefore our freedom to be with God and others in the world in a proper economy of being and relation towards such a horizon.

It is God who remains free in relation to sin, free to draw it into a future and therefore to refuse it any primary reality (just as it is God who really bears the cost of sin and it is only by looking at God on the cross that we can arrive at an adequate appreciation of the depths of our situation and its seriousness). Therefore God's freedom is also our own, and it is only in God's freedom in relation to our bondage to sin that we may have hope of liberation. We are not free to be our own help in this situation, but, in God's grace, God has given Godself to be our help. And we are called in our freedom to be God's help in the project of our own liberation.

---

[43] Edward Farley, *Good and Evil: Interpreting a Human Condition* (Minneapolis: Fortress, 1990), p.136.

5. Imago Libertatis: Human and Divine Freedom

Christoph Schwöbel

I. Freedom The Modern Universal

Thesis 1: Freedom is the fundamental principle for understanding what it means to be human in the modern (and post-modern) era. As such it serves as the ultimate warrant for human actions, desires and interests and as the fundamental reference-point for the justification of our actions, desires and interests. Therefore in the modern era challenging the fundamental role of freedom always takes the form of criticizing one concept of freedom by arguing for another.

To say that freedom is the fundamental principle of understanding what it means to be human in the modern era is almost a platitude. But like some platitudes this one seems to have hidden depths which are well worth exploring. Among the three catch-words of the French Revolution, *liberté*, *égalité* and *fraternité*, *liberté*, freedom, is the one that has proved to be the dominant and historically victorious principle. For a long time it appeared as if demands for justice, understood as equality, provided an equally strong claim for dominance, at least in the political realm. However, the breakdown of the régimes of state socialism in the last few years seems to indicate that a notion of equality which is not based on a strong affirmation of freedom has in its practical forms of realization only a limited historical life-span. The apparent dialectic between the demands of freedom and the demands of social justice understood as equality according to which an increase of freedom for some always implies a decrease of justice for the rest seems to have been historically resolved in such a way that equality is now interpreted almost universally as equal access to the exercise of freedom. Freedom appears as the fundamental principle, justice as equality as a derivative notion.

With this dominance of the postulate of freedom, the third principle of the French Revolution becomes elusive. What could it mean to live as free and equal brothers and sisters when equality is defined in terms of freedom and the comradeship of the interna-

tional solidarity of socialism has made way for a diversity of
national and cultural liberation movements that can form tactical
coalitions, but can no longer produce a vision of brotherhood and
sisterhood in its local, regional and universal dimensions?

The dominant role of freedom as the fundamental principle for
understanding what it means to be human has a number of
interesting consequences. On the surface, everybody can experience the fact that the rhetoric of freedom has reached a stage of
hyper-inflation. Every form of argument, every form of persuasion
has to make reference to freedom in order to have a chance of
succeeding. The advertising industry offers the most glaring
examples. Even the attempt at patent manipulation seems to
work only if it is based on an appeal to our freedom — a lesson
totalitarian régimes all over the world have learned well in this
century. This implies, of course, that we are willing and able to
suspend our critical judgement for quite a long time provided the
attempt to persuade us is based on an appeal to our freedom,
allegedly the foundation of our capacity for critical judgement.
That appeals to freedom can become part of a strategy of deception
and perhaps even self-deception shows that there seems to be a
curious connection between the centrality and dominance of the
concept of freedom and its opacity. The more dominant freedom
becomes for our self-understanding, the hazier the notion of
freedom seems to become and the more ambiguous are the uses of
the rhetoric of freedom.

The dominance of the notion of freedom for human self-understanding in the modern era seems to be the result of a progressive
process of radicalization in the interpretation of the concept of
freedom. The most fundamental stage in conceiving freedom
theoretically and practically is liberation from external coercion
and domination, the fight for the right of freedom from oppression
through external agencies which may attempt to assert their
domination by force or by externally imposed authority. This fight
for freedom from external domination is rightly seen as a fundamental human right, as an inalienable aspect of human dignity.
However, once external oppression in its most glaring forms is
removed, the process of freedom continues. The situation where
one's choices are no longer determined by external agencies
through external means challenges one to find a strategy of
determining one's own goals and means of action. And at this stage
it is discovered that when the external forces of oppression have
been removed there still remain internal authorities to be dealt
with, the heteronomous determination through authorities which
we internalize, traditions, customs, prescriptive concepts and
behaviour codes which may restrict our freedom just as oppres-
sively as external agencies.

The discovery of interiority, the dimension of the internal life of our beliefs, norms of action and desires has much to do with becoming conscious of heteronomous domination within ourselves. Once we move beyond this stage the understanding of freedom changes quite dramatically. Now the issues are no longer liberation from external domination or emancipation from heteronomous determination of our personal identity through internalized authorities. The main question is not: How can I gain freedom from whatever restricts my freedom? but: *What* do I want to be free *for*? Freedom is extended to the realm of self-interpretation, it becomes the central focus of self-expression. We have moved from the use of freedom as a critical concept defined by its opposition against restrictive and oppressive agencies to the use of freedom as a constructive concept where our self-interpretation becomes a form of self-expression. There are no longer given alternatives between which we have to choose. Choice has become absolute, because it also extends to choices between interpretations of our choices. According to some of the practitioners of moral philosophy we have come to this stage in present day discussions of ethics. Not only are policies of action seen as the object of choice, not only has our moral character become subject to our creative self-interpretation, but the moral theories themselves, the strategies of justifying our choices, have become objects of choice.

It seems that in our industrialized countries in Western Europe and North America, and increasingly in Eastern Europe, and perhaps all over the world, we have arrived at the stage where freedom is conceived in this radical sense. Even if this analysis is not entirely correct, there are two elements of this situation which are important for our reflections. First of all, where the notion of freedom has become culturally so dominant and where it is understood in such a radical sense, the concept of freedom itself becomes opaque and requires clarification. But, secondly, where freedom has achieved this central position for our self-understanding it seems to lead to the situation that every critical reflection on our theory and practice of freedom presents itself as a critique of one conception of freedom by another. The following reflections are no exception.

Thesis 2: The concept of freedom expresses a fundamental feature of human beings as agents, as originators of intentional action. It depicts the actuality of intentional action in which agents choose certain goals and means of action, and decide to follow certain norms of action. Furthermore, it describes the actuality of freedom as being rooted in the capacity of freedom which is, as a constitutive part of human personal being, part of its ontological constitution.

The impressionistic sketch I have attempted of some significant aspects of the modern understanding of freedom requires clarification of some of the basic aspects of the concept because it focused on the dominance of the concept of freedom for human self-understanding and the concomitant radicalization of freedom. This attempt at clarification cannot but start from basics. The first of the basic features which we have to observe here is that the concept of freedom describes human beings as agents. It is in the correlation of freedom and intentional action that freedom (and intentional action) is defined. To talk of an occurrence as an act means to identify an agent as the main cause of the happening of the occurrence. We see the agent as the originator of his or her actions so that the occurrence can be ascribed to the agent as his or her act, so that agents can be held responsible for their actions. Acts are seen as free actions if their occurrence cannot be sufficiently explained in terms of necessary and sufficient conditions which give agents only a secondary contributory role in bringing about a certain event, but ascribe the determinative role for the bringing about of an event to the agent's intention. Freedom is thus in a very rudimentary sense understood as an agent's capacity for intentional action, for selecting certain goals of actions, means of action and certain action-regulating norms of action, be they of a technical or a moral nature. The notion of freedom addresses the situation of an agent as an originator of actions (and not merely as a medium for the transmission of the effects of certain natural causes), and by referring to the agent's intention describes this situation primarily from the perspective of the agent.

If the concept of freedom is understood in the context of intentional action, then the range of actions comprised under this concept extend not only to our physical activity and our organizational activity, but also to our interpretative acts. Wherever semiotic activity, the use of signs, is involved, wherever there is interpretative activity, freedom is involved. We do not passively receive experiences, we *make* experiences by the active synthesis of bringing together sense perceptions and interpretative words and concepts. Interpretative action is presupposed in the physical and organizational action by which we effect changes in the world. It is through our interpretation of the world and of ourselves as agents in the world by means of various images, metaphors, concepts and models that the world is constituted as a world of experience, that is as a field of action.[1] In its description of the

---

[1]   For a fuller account of the concept of experience see my *God: Action and Revelation* (Kampen: Kok Pharos Publishing House, 1992), pp.103-12.

world, interpretative action defines for us the possibilities of action, presents us with possible goals and aims of action and enables us to formulate norms of action which we can adopt. It is important to see that freedom is by no means restricted to a choice between given alternatives. Which choices we recognize in a given situation of action depends already on our interpretative action which is just as much intentional action as the physical or organizational action of effecting changes in the external world. Freedom is therefore not to be restricted to the capacity of doing this rather than that. The primary seat of freedom is the selection of certain goals of action and the interpretative action that enables us to make such a selection.

When the actuality of freedom is interpreted in this comprehensive sense, it cannot be understood as a contingent property of human being but must be seen as constitutive for what it means to be human. And this is to be understood in the strong sense of the ontological constitution of being human, of what it means to be a human person. Freedom appears in this way as the primary ontological distinction of human being. This should not preclude the question whether it is not also possible to speak of freedom in other contexts, with regard to animal behaviour or the interrelation of spontaneity and law-governed structures in nature. What is, however, asserted is that no understanding of human being can be complete that does not give freedom a constitutive part in defining what it means to be human.

Two of the major shifts which distinguish modern thought from pre-modern thought can be seen as expressions of the constitutive role of freedom for human being. The first is the turn from substance to subject, the shift in focusing attention not primarily on an ordered cosmos of substances which can be seen as existing in a fixed ontological order but on the subject, so that reflection on being starts not from reflection on what is out there, but from the subject of reflection. The constitutive role of freedom for human being could not be more effectively illustrated than by concentrating on human acts of freedom as the focus of ontological reflection. The second turn is closely related to the first one. It is the shift from ontology to epistemology. When we focus our attention on the subject of reflection, the first question is not 'What is this and as what can it be classified in the order of being?', but 'How can I know that this is this, what are the conditions for the possibility of identifying and predicating it as something?' The question of the experience of reality becomes the question of the reality of experience, and if it is true that experience is actively constituted by our acts of synthesis, the freedom presupposed in this activity is the primary reality. It is perhaps no exaggeration to say that a continuing theme of the debates of modern philosophy is the attempt at clarifying the role of freedom for our understanding of reality.

Thesis 3: In the modern context freedom is interpreted as the capacity for self-determination. In choosing to perform certain acts rather than others, in deciding for certain goals, means and norms of action rather than others, human beings always choose themselves. This process is programmatically expressed in the concept of autonomy as self-legislation. While this notion functioned in its original context in Kantian philosophy as a controlling concept (choosing to follow the correct universalizable moral maxim over against other desires and motivations), it functions, when this moral restriction is lifted, as a creative strategy of self-constitution: I will be who I choose to be. If freedom is interpreted and practised in this radical sense it is treated as an absolute and as, in principle, if not in practice, infinite freedom.

The basic elements of the understanding of freedom that we have so far characterized are interpreted in the context of modernity in a very specific sense. This sense is aptly summarized in the concept of autonomy which as one of the key-concepts of the modern understanding of freedom has gained a permanent significance which has survived the theories in which it was originally incorporated. The notion of autonomy rests on the observation that in our free intentional action, we not only effect changes in our environment. When we take decisions which reach beyond the range of concrete alternatives of limited significance, and which affect our further policies of actions, our choices can be interpreted as instances of self-determination.[2] In deciding for policies of action which incorporate choices concerning the inter-

---

[2] The difference and relationship between freedom from coercion and freedom as self-determination is clearly brought out by a contrast between Thomas Hobbes and Baruch Spinoza. Hobbes maintains an understanding of freedom where freedom is essentially *absentia impedimentorum motus* (cf. *De cive*, c. 9, sect. 9), understood as the absence of physical coercion. Spinoza starts from the same concept, but interprets it in a metaphysical sense: *libertas a coactione* means to be determined exclusively by the necessity of one's nature, i.e. to be completely self-determined: 'Ea res libera dicitur, quae ex sola suae naturae necessitate existit, et a se sola ad agendum determinatur' (*Ethica* I, def. 7). Whereas Spinoza insists that only God can be called free in this sense, it is the particular dynamic of the modern development of the understanding of freedom that this notion is transferred to the individual human being.

pretation of our possibilities of action, of our goals of action and of the norms of action we attempt to observe, we decide the fundamental orientation of our lives. Such decisions are examples of self-determination. Self-determination is contrasted to determination by external authorities. It is this contrast which is brought out in the opposition of the concepts of autonomy and heteronomy. Whereas heteronomy denotes the restriction of our self-determination through an external, alien determinative influence, autonomy describes the use of freedom as self-determination as a process of self-legislation.

In the original context of application in Kant's moral philosophy, the ancient correlation of law (*nomos*) and freedom is redefined in such a sense that the law no longer defines external limits of freedom, but that free agents determine for themselves the internal norms of action they observe in the exercise of their freedom. The radical nature of this step consists in two major elements: the concept of law is no longer applied to an external positive conception of laws, but to the internal process of self-legislation. And, furthermore, the moral character of that law is no longer given in a specific content — certain material prohibitions or goals of action defined by their content — but in a formal rule, expressed in the rule of universalizability, that the norm applied in moral self-legislation should be able to function as a universal moral law, interpreted on the analogy of a law of nature.[3] It must, however, be noted that the concept of autonomy as a specific interpretation of self-determination in freedom functions as a controlling concept, as a critical concept applied to our desires, our interests and motivations. Autonomy in this critical sense presupposes a stable understanding of what human nature is which underlies the test of the universalizability of our norms of action. The formalism of the Kantian notion of freedom as autonomy presupposes an implicit consensus about the nature and the destiny of humanity.

We are now in a situation where this consensus can no longer be implicitly presupposed. We encounter a great cultural, social diversity of notions of what it means to be human, whose only common denominator seems to be the appeal to the notion of freedom as self-determination as a constitutive element of the nature of humanity. We can no longer, as Kant could, provide a

---

[3]   This can most clearly be seen in the first two versions of the categorical imperative in *Grundlegung zur Metaphysik der Sitten* (1785): 'handle nur nach derjenigen Maxime, durch die du zugleich wollen kannst, daß sie ein allgemeines Gesetz werde' and 'handle so, als ob die Maxime deiner Handlung durch deinen Willen zum allgemeinen Naturgesetze werden sollte' (Hamburg: Felix Meiner, 1965), pp.42 and 43.

clear answer to the questions 'For whom would a given norm of action function as a universal moral law and by whom could it be recognized as such?' In such a situation of pluralism concerning our most basic concepts and understandings the rule of universalizability seems to be no longer able to function as an infallible test of morality and the notion of autonomy loses its critical, controlling function. For Kant, the sovereignty of freedom was very much a constitutional monarchy, firmly self-restricted by the demands of the iron law of the categorical imperative. Where the underlying basic assumptions about the nature of humanity and the universality of human reason have become questionable, there is a tendency for freedom to take a more autocratic form. What we are experiencing in such a situation is a transformation of the understanding of freedom as autonomy from a critical notion to a constructive ideal. Freedom as self-determination is, it seems, radically interpreted as self-constitution: 'I will be who I choose to be' becomes the new culturally accepted creed. Freedom is no longer seen as relative to a moral law, albeit only the formal rule of universalizability, but as self-determination, it is seen as relative only to itself and so becomes absolute as self-constitution. The moral boundaries which Kant attempted to build into the notion of freedom have fallen and it becomes, at least in principle, limitless, infinite.

I want to suggest that this is the understanding of freedom which is to a large extent operative in our culture which has in consequence become a culture of self-constitution and self-fulfilment. According to the tacit creed which informs the life of our societies we are all, or at least we should be, self-made men and women. One would have to go to far greater lengths of cultural analysis and sociological research in order to substantiate such a thesis.[4] I offer it merely as a suggestion which is capable of giving

---

[4] It could, of course, be objected that the sketch developed here focuses too much on modernity and does not sufficiently take into account the alleged shift to the situation of post-modernism. I am uncertain whether one can indeed speak of a shift from the 'modern' to the 'post-modern' because it seems questionable whether one can without much more extensive analysis transfer a concept from the history and theory of architecture to the cultural situation as a whole without losing much of its descriptive value. There is much to be said for the alternative theory of 'reflexive modernization' developed by the sociologist Ulrich Beck, *Die Erfindung des Politischen* (Frankfurt: Suhrkamp, 1993), especially pp.57-98, which describes the new state of society as one brought about by the latent by-products of the victory of modernity.

Regardless of the stance one takes in this issue, it would still seem that the described process of the radicalization of the notion of freedom

a rough interpretation of a number of cultural developments which we all observe and experience in the rhetoric that accompanies them and in the crises they produce in individual lives and in the state of our societies as a whole.

II. The Contradictions of Freedom

Thesis 4: The modern self-interpretation of freedom contains ambiguities which can lead in theory and in practice to decisive self-contradictions which, in turn, present a threat to freedom.

We have seen in our analysis of the concept of freedom that freedom presupposes power, the capacity to bring about the effects we intend to realize. This power requires control of the circumstances of action so that our means of action are sufficient to establish a causal link between our intentions and our goals of action. In order to exercise this control, it is necessary that we distinguish between what we can do and what we are unable to do. The ambiguity consists in the fact that power is necessary for the exercise of freedom, but that there is a fine balance between power to act successfully and an assumption of power that may threaten our capacity to act successfully. Where we have exaggerated expectations concerning our capacity to control the circumstances of our action, the ensuing disappointments may lead to severe crises of our trust in our capacity for free intentional action.

The rhetoric of the modern self-understanding of freedom as unlimited autonomy presents us with a vision of the empowerment of the human agent which may create such unrealistic

is one of the elements of continuity between whatever stages or epochs one distinguishes. On this point, I agree with the analysis Charles Taylor gives in *Sources of the Self* (Cambridge: Cambridge University Press, 1989) of the work of post-modern theorists such as Derrida and Lyotard. With regard to the all-encompassing character of the process of deconstruction in Derrida, Taylor writes: 'Nothing emerges from this flux worth affirming, and so what in fact comes to be celebrated is the deconstructing power itself, the prodigious power of subjectivity to undo all the potential allegiances which might bind it; pure untrammelled freedom' (p.489). This is Taylor's concluding verdict: 'The "post-modernism" of Lyotard turns out to be an over-elaborated boost for the first spiritual profile of modernism, in the name of unrestricted freedom. The work of Derrida and Foucault ... also fits within this first profile. They offer charters for subjectivism and the celebration of our own creative power at the cost of occluding what is spiritually arresting in this whole movement of contemporary culture' (p.490).

expectations concerning our capacity to exercise control over the circumstances of our actions that we experience a failure to act successfully as a severe crisis of our freedom. The assumption of unlimited power may lead to such strong experiences of powerlessness that we attempt to retreat from the role of being agents altogether. The agent becomes a patient. The tragic aspect of this crisis of freedom is that this retreat is, in fact, impossible. We cannot but act, in the sense that even our refusal to act creates effects, after-effects and side-effects, just as actions do. There is no retreat from the responsibility of freedom, but there can be the despair of disenchanted freedom from which there is no escape into a non-acting part in the human drama.

We encounter similar phenomena with regard to the knowledge that is presupposed in our intentional action. The exercise of freedom requires that we have knowledge about our capacities of action, of our intentions and motives, of our means of action, our goals of action and the possible and probable effects, after-effects and side-effects of our actions. In order to generate reliable policies of action the modern rhetoric of absolute freedom requires comprehensive knowledge of all these aspects of action. But, in fact, our knowledge is limited. It is not only quantitatively limited, but qualitatively limited in that it is mediated through our social forms of existence and the physical processes of our interaction with our environment. The modern rhetoric of freedom persuades us to ignore these limitations of our action-directing knowledge systematically and thus encourages an epistemic arrogance which presents us with an image of absolute controlling knowledge of our actions. Where the exaggerated expectations this notion creates are disappointed, this may not only lead to a readjustment of the claims made for the range and character of our knowledge but to a general, almost unrestricted, scepticism. This, in turn, has the effect that our actions are no longer determined by confidence in our action-directing knowledge, but tend to become arbitrary, since the disappointment of the expectations of unlimited knowledge leads to a general lack of trust in the capacity of our knowledge to direct our actions, and this comes close to indifference.

There is a similar phenomenon of self-contradiction concerning the temporality of our actions. Human actions occur in time and in order to be successful require adaptation to the temporal circumstances of our actions. Otherwise our actions may trigger long-term effects which are out of our control and may cancel out the short-term results we intended in the first place. Human responsibility is closely tied to observance of the temporality of ourselves as agents and our actions. Again, it seems that the modern rhetoric of freedom suggests that we ignore this temporality systematically, so that we are confronted with the long-term effects of our actions which occur beyond the time-span we can influence or control. There are many examples of our actions producing long-term effects that cancel out their intended short-term benefits. The legacy left to future generations by DDT spraying campaigns or by the long-lasting radiation levels of nuclear waste have brought this sharply to our attention. The image of ourselves as eternal agents which the rhetoric of freedom suggests produces effects which confront us painfully with our temporal existence. Where our actions seem to have uncontrollable long-term effects beyond our own life-span, there is the danger that the responsibility for our actions will be eroded, and human agents will be seen as tragic figures condemned to act, but constantly overtaken by unforeseen and unintended consequences of their actions.

The contradictions of freedom which are provoked by the conceptions of freedom as absolute, unlimited and sovereign are genuine self-contradictions insofar as they imply illusory expectations concerning fundamental aspects which, when they are disappointed, restrict our freedom to the point of incapacitating intentional action. In this respect, the consequences of the modern rhetoric of absolute freedom are not very different from those of a radically deterministic picture of the world and the role of human agents in it. There is a wide range of phenomena where these self-contradictions of freedom can be experienced. Two of the most significant are the relationship between our human sociality and our selfhood, and our relationship to the natural world.

Thesis 5: Where freedom is understood as self-constitution, it runs the risk of having as its consequences self-loss and the loss of the other, since it denies the relational constitution of human personal identity.

We have sketched the process in which freedom as the capacity for self-determination is radicalized to such a degree that it extends to the constitution of freedom, so that freedom is radically understood as self-constituted. Freedom is seen as truly autonomous where it is relative only to itself and thus absolute. If, in addition, freedom is seen as the fundamental notion for what it means to be a human person, human personal identity must consequently be understood as the result of self-constitutive acts of the human subject.

Selfhood and identity are notions which express a fundamental difference between the human person and its identity as a self and the personal and non-personal environment which is non-self, different from the self. This difference of the particularity of identity, however, presupposes relation, the relationship in which human persons exist to other persons and through which the difference of personal particularity is mediated. Kierkegaard's thesis that the human person is a relationship which relates to itself[5] brings that out very clearly: personal identity is a relationship to ourselves which presupposes our relatedness to other people. This relatedness is prior to our active relations to ourselves and others. Personal identity presupposes personal relations which are given before we can actively assert our self-identity. The spontaneity of self-assertion presupposes the receptivity of relationships in which others act towards us. In the narrative of identity formation we are first passive insofar as other persons address us as particular persons before we can assert our personal identity by actively relating to the relatedness which we receive. The mutuality of personal social relations is presupposed in the affirmation of our self-identity.[6]

If this description of the connections between identity and sociality, between self affirmation and mutuality, between spontaneity and receptivity is correct then the modern rhetoric of freedom as self-constitution of the self must be interpreted as the denial of the presuppositions of personal identity which are not constituted *by* us, but *for* us. Where the role of the other person is denied in the constitution of personal freedom, the attempted self-constitution of freedom leads to self-loss. It is therefore not very surprising that Augustine's phenomenology of sin as *superbia, concupiscentia* and *amor sui* still seems to provide the categories for the psychopathology of the self-constituted ego and its crises.[7]

Thesis 6: The interpretation of freedom as self-constitution leads into the perilous situation that the relationship of the human agent to the world threatens to effect the destruction of the natural world and thus puts the natural bases of human life at risk.

5   *Sygdommen til Døden [Sickness Unto Death]* (1849), *Samlede Vaerker* XI, p.127.
6   For a more systematic account see 'Human Being as Relational Being: Twelve Theses for a Christian Anthropology', in: C. Schwöbel & C. E. Gunton (eds), *Persons, Divine and Human* (Edinburgh: T&T Clark, 1991), pp.141-65.
7   On Augustine, Erich Dinkler, *Die Anthropologie Augustins* (Stuttgart: Kohlhammer, 1934) still provides a reliable guide. The influence of Augustine's doctrine of sin in contemporary discussion is discussed by Wolfhart Pannenberg, *Systematische Theologie II* (Göttingen: Vandenhoek & Ruprecht, 1991), pp.277-93.

Where freedom is understood as self-constituted, the relationship of the human agents to everything outside themselves is seen as a constructive relationship. This is expressed with admirable precision by the philosopher J. G. Fichte who attempts to find a foundation for all knowledge in the self-positing act of the ego and consequently describes the relationship of the ego to the world as one where the ego posits the world as the self-limitation of the ego.[8] Although this view appears as the most radical expression of the idealist creed, it nevertheless seems to illustrate one of the fundamental aspects of the modern relationship of humans to the natural world in industrialized countries. Much of the relationship to the natural world seems to be governed by a principle of free and unrestrained creativity, of building a new world, a meta-cosmos of human artefacts in which the givenness of the natural order is seen as an impediment to human world construction which needs to be subdued and overcome. The environmental crisis has confronted us with the effects of a human relationship to the world of nature that is interpreted as defined by seemingly unlimited creative freedom. The assumption of a wholly constructive relationship to the natural world has been disclosed as a largely destructive relationship. The self-contradiction of freedom becomes obvious where the destructiveness of this creative relationship is experienced as self-destructive. Not only is our freedom in relating to the natural order radically restricted by the results of the exercise of unrestricted freedom, so that in many cases it is limited to strategies of damage limitation, but the natural bases for the survival of human life and with that of human freedom, are themselves under threat.[9]

What the interpretation of freedom as self-constitutive and therefore radically creative freedom overlooks is that human agents are, as embodied agents, bound by many links into the order of the natural world. The attempt at subduing and dominating the natural order in the pursuit of the aims of human creativity leads to the situation where it seems that the natural world is striking back at the human violators of its order, threatening the

---

[8]   On Fichte see the instructive chapter, 'J. G. Fichte and J. W. F. Schelling' by John Heywood Thomas in *Nineteenth Century Religious Thought in the West*, vol.I, edited by N. Smart, J. Clayton, S. Katz and P. Sherry (Cambridge: Cambridge University Press, 1985), pp.41-80. He also shows how the first principle of the *Wissenschaftslehre* that I refer to is related to Fichte's religious thought.

[9]   See Günter Altner, *Die Überlebenskrise in der Gegenwart. Ansätze zum Dialog mit der Natur in Naturwissenschaft und Theologie* (Darmstadt: Wissenschaftliche Buchgesellschaft, 1987).

continued existence of the human race. As embodied agents we are dependent on being able to effect physical changes in the world and on employing the matter and structures of the natural world as means to achieve our purposes. The fatal mistakes occur where human agents ignore the effects of the construction of the meta-cosmos of human creativity on the cosmos of the natural order, and act as if the worth of the natural world is exclusively defined by the ways in which it can be instrumentalized for the achievement of human aims. Since the exercise of human freedom is dependent on the functioning order of the natural world in many ways, the destruction of this natural world for the sake of constructing a world in our image undermines the bases of human life and the natural bases of human freedom. Human agents who violate the order of nature become patients forced to suffer the consequences of their actions together with the suffering non-human creation.

III. Freedom and the Denial of God

Thesis 7: The absolutism of human freedom which appears as the denial of God is (historically and systematically) dependent on an image of divine freedom.

So far we have discussed, without any explicit reference to religious beliefs and theological thought, almost *etsi Deus non daretur* — as if there were no God — aspects and trends of modern interpretations in theory and practice, sketching a picture with many generalizations that should help us to identify some tendencies in our understanding of freedom.[10] This seems only appropriate to our theme because the history of the radicalization of the interpretation of human freedom which we have sketched in some of its aspects and contradictions is also the history of different stages of taking leave of God. The process of the radicalization of the conception of human freedom and the process of the denial of God in modern thought seem to be parallel developments. One can study that in many of the conceptions of radical freedom. Modern atheism is in many ways an atheism for the sake of human freedom. Where human freedom is seen as absolute, a God who is claimed to be absolute can only appear as a threat to freedom. This is not only true of the theoretical atheism of some philosophers, but also of the practical atheism that is a significant feature of our

---

[10] It is still illuminating to compare Dietrich Bonhoeffer's use of this formula by Hugo Grotius, in *Widerstand und Ergebung* (München: Chr. Kaiser Verlag, 1952), pp.240ff.

contemporary societies. In passing, we can observe that the parallels between the theoretical atheism of philosophical thinkers in the nineteenth century and the practical atheism of the twentieth century indicate that it is a mistake to assume that academic philosophers are safely locked away in their ivory towers where they conduct their thought experiments without the risk of contaminating what happens in the real world. Reflection on the theme of freedom shows quite clearly that what may begin in the seclusion of the ivory tower may finish on the market-place of largely implicit practical views of life.

In spite of this connection between the affirmation of radical freedom and the denial of God in the modern history of the interpretation of freedom, we find that there is nevertheless a cluster of theological motifs operative in this process which is most appropriately interpreted as an image of divine freedom. In the radical interpretation of human freedom we find freedom interpreted in a series of attributes which point to specific divine attributes. This link can be established in many ways, historically and systematically. Where freedom is interpreted in terms of the power of the agent which is not restricted by external agencies but only through the self-regulation of the agent, we encounter a conception of power which conceives of omnipotence as the *potentia absoluta* which is only self-restricted as *potentia ordinata* in God's relationship to the creation.[11] The heritage of nominalism, where this distinction, which we already find in Thomas Aquinas, became programmatic, becomes clear where the human agent is no longer understood as integrated into a given order of being, but constitutes this order in free acts of interpretation and organization. Where the action-directing knowledge of the agents is understood in terms of the active constitution of knowledge through the agents' intellect, and the agents' knowledge of their capacities of action is interpreted as immediate, we are confronted with a conception of knowledge which is understood in terms of divine omniscience. When the unlimited character of human freedom is interpreted in such a way that the temporal character of human agency is ignored, human agents are informed by a notion of the agents' possession of their time which is, at least, highly reminiscent of divine eternity. The similarities do not stop at the appropriation of specific divine attributes; they also extend to the radical interpretation of the mode of being of freedom. Where freedom is interpreted as self-constituted, recourse is taken to *aseitas* as the mode of being in which God is understood as *causa*

---

[11] See Gijsbert van den Brink, *Almighty God* (Kampen: Kok Pharos Publishing House, 1993).

sui. The conceptuality of self-constitution is, in its application to human freedom, directly borrowed from the attempt to distinguish the mode of being of God as the wholly self-explanatory being which is the ultimate explanation of everything that is not God. From this, it is only a small step to interpreting the relation of human creativity to the world on the analogy of the sovereign relationship of God to a world which is created *ex nihilo*.

The thesis I want to suggest on the basis of these similarities is that the process of the radicalization of freedom which characterizes modernity is shaped by a specific image of divine freedom which is understood as omnipotent, omniscient, eternal, self-constituted and absolutely creative. This can also explain why the radicalization of the understanding of freedom went hand in hand with the modern history of atheism. Where human freedom is fashioned after the image of divine freedom the existence of God must be denied for the sake of radical human freedom.

Thesis 8: The notion of an image which is operative in the modern radicalization of freedom is that of image as imitation *which can result in the substitution of the reality that is imaged by the reality of the image.*

That freedom is the *imago Dei* in humanity is an idea which has had a firm place in the theological tradition since Bernard of Clairvaux (1090-1153) defended it in his tract *De diligendo Dei* and gave it a systematic explication in his *Tractatus de gratia et libero arbitrio*. Bernard distinguishes carefully between the freedom of the will (*libertas arbitrii*) which is the image (*imago*) of God's freedom in humanity and the freedom of good counsel (*libertas consilii*), the wisdom to deliberate which means will be expedient for realizing one's choice, which corresponds to divine wisdom, and the freedom of inclination (*libertas complaciti*), the affective capacity or power to take pleasure in what one deems to be good, which in turn corresponds to divine omnipotence. However, the latter two forms of freedom are part of the *similitudo Dei* which distinguished human being in Paradise, but was lost in the Fall. The purpose of salvation is for Bernard the reconstitution of the original state of humanity which he describes as a process of *reformatio* which occurs *sola gratia* without a contribution of the freedom of the will. The dynamics of this process is, in keeping with Bernard's christological mysticism, described in terms of Christ's relationship to us: *in Christo, per Christum* and *cum Christo*. First, we have been created in Christ for freedom of the will; second, we are reformed through Christ in the Spirit of freedom; and then, we will be perfected with Christ in the state of eternity: *'primo namque in Christo creati in libertatem voluntatis, secundo reformamur per Christum in spiritum libertatis, cum Christo deinde consummandi in statum aeternitatis.'*[12] In the philosophies of the seventeenth and eighteenth centuries, when the notion of the image of God became dominant in determining the attitude of philosophers in describing human interaction with reality, as Edward Craig has shown in his fascinating and provocative book *The Mind of God and the Works of Man*,[13] the sophisticated distinctions which Bernard makes along with the tradition are ignored. The rise of philosophical theism, which attempted to provide a rational defence for basic religious and moral beliefs in order to establish a common ground of religious and moral orientation in societies torn apart by the religious wars and threatened by religious scepticism,[14] may have further contributed to disregarding the links which bind the notion of humanity as created in the image of God into the conceptual scheme of Christian beliefs. The distinction between *imago* and *similitudo* which interprets the notion in terms of the narrative of fall, redemption and salvation is ignored, and the motif is employed in the simplified form which Craig appropriately calls the Similarity Thesis. There is a quantitative difference between the mind of God and the human mind, but qualitative identity. This is further developed by thinkers like Leibniz who attempted to conquer the Enlightenment by means of its own intellectual armoury. Leibniz explicitly confirms the thesis of quantitative difference and qualitative identity: 'For it can be said that created minds differ from God only as lesser from greater, as finite from infinite.'[15] The Similarity Thesis applies not only to our knowledge, Leibniz argues, but also to our actions: '... one spirit alone is worth a whole world since it not merely expresses the world but also knows it and conducts itself in it after the fashion

---

[12] *Tract. de grat.*, 14.49. The critical edition of *De gratia et libero arbitrio* can be found in J. Leclerq, *S. Bernardi opera III* (Rome: editiones Cistercienses, 1963), pp.165-203. Cf. the English edition *On Grace and Free Choice (de gratia et libero arbitrio) by Bernard of Clairvaux*, translated by Daniel O'Donovan OCSO, with an introduction by B. McGinn, (Kalamazoo, Michigan: Cistercian Publications, 1988).

[13] Edward Craig, *The Mind of God and the Works of Man* (Oxford: Oxford University Press, 1987).

[14] Cf. my essay 'After Post-Theism', in: Svend Andersen (ed.), *Theism: Tradition and Modernity* (Aarhus: Aarhus University Press, 1994), pp.157-91, especially pp.168-76.

[15] G. W. Leibniz, letter to Arnauld, 9 October 1687, cited in Craig, *The Mind of God*, p.51.

of God.'[16] And in this respect the image of God is interpreted in terms of imitation, and in Leibniz explicitly related to the divine perfections, so that one can say of a substance in Leibniz's monadological metaphysics: '... that it extends its power over all the others in imitation of the omnipotence of the Creator.'[17]
The interpretation of humanity as the image of God which differs from God quantitatively, but not qualitatively, and which consists in imitating the divine perfections, assumes a direct connection, which is not dependent on the christological mediation of the image of God in humanity which we have noted in Bernard, between what is imaged and the image. When the image of God is interpreted in terms of quantitative difference as imitation of divine perfections, image turns into substitution where it can be shown that human activity is not dependent on prevenient divine action. This point is reached where human freedom is interpreted as autonomy, not merely as self-legislation but as self-constitution of the human agent. Once this step is taken the quantitative difference becomes irrelevant, the image expresses only its own reality and we have become gods. The promise 'eritis sicut Deus': you will be like God, has been fulfilled.

Thesis 9: The attempt to appropriate divine freedom contains for human agents the potentiality for the dehumanization of the human, and presents radical freedom as an escape into unaccountability.

There is a long tradition going back to Psalm 8 which presents the place of human beings in the created order as being on the boundary, lower than the angels, higher than the beasts. Human beings are understood as the meeting-place between the spiritual and the material, the borderland between the realm of freedom and the realm of necessity. The traditions of Christianity have in many ways interpreted this position as one of special distinction expressed by the metaphor of the image of God and specifically

[16] Leibniz, *Discourse on Metphysics*, XXXVI, cited in Craig, *The Mind of God*, p.52. It would not seem inappropriate to interpret the development of this thought in Leibniz in such a way that he ascibes to humans not only Bernard's *libertas arbitrii* but also the *libertas consilii* and the *libertas complaciti* ('knows it and conducts itself in it after the fashion of God'). This indicates that Bernard's distinction between *imago* and *similitudo* is systematically ignored in this context. This is the condition for interpreting the image of God in terms of imitation.
[17] Leibniz, *Discourse on Metaphysics* IX, cited in Craig, *The Mind of God*, p.58.

vindicated by the Incarnation. But this position is also interpreted as an unstable location exposed to the temptations of sin and the dark shadows of the gift of freedom. It is, moreover, described, perhaps most poignantly in the narrative of the Fall, as one which cannot be maintained by human beings so that humans are dislocated in the created order, and experience God and the world that surrounds them as a threat to their existence.[18] The preservation of the specifically human seems to be intricately connected to maintaining this position on the boundary, the point of contact between the being of the creator and the created order. Modern anthropology has in many ways confirmed this view, which can be found in many biblical traditions and throughout the history of Christianity, by speaking of the human capacity for self-transcendence which finds its expression in that human openness to the world which is both the glory and the curse of humanity.[19] Where human being is dislocated in the relational order of creation, it cannot fall back upon the safely established mechanisms which enable the survival of animal life.

The instability of the place of humans in the created order finds its most troubling, and perhaps tragic, expression in the dialectics of human self-transcendence. When humans aspire to be more than human, their consequent dislocation in the relational order of created being brings them to being less then human. And even in this state we do not achieve a second innocence of animal grace, the consonance of our instincts with our environment, but the curse of unrelatedness, of the atomistic existence of the dislocated and therefore empty self. Tendencies of dehumanization which we observe in history do not begin with the avowed striving to a lower level of existence, of escaping the burden of freedom by being submerged in the mechanism of stimulus and response, but with striving for a higher level of existence, transcending the level of the merely human. It is no accident that the most horrendous atrocities our century has seen occurred against the background of the (however misinterpreted) rhetoric of Nietzsche's superman.

---

[18] For a more extensive development of the interpretation of the Fall as *dislocation*, see my article 'Human Being as Relational Being', in: Schwöbel and Gunton, *Persons, Divine and Human*, pp.141-65.

[19] This aspect is systematically developed by Wolfhart Pannenberg in *Anthropology in Theological Perspective*, translated by Matthew J. O'Connell (Edinburgh: T&T Clark, 1985). See also my review article 'Theology in Anthropological Perspective?' *King's Theological Review* X (1987), 21-5.

It is therefore not surprising to find that the radical conception of freedom as absolute and unlimited lies at the heart of many of the most dehumanizing tendencies we observe in modern history. Where freedom is seen as radically self-constituted, responsibility is restricted to the responsibility of agents to themselves, and it is at this point that the claim of radical autonomy cannot be distinguished from the escape into unaccountability. This, however, dissolves the notion of intentional agency which is the basis for the modern understanding of freedom altogether, because this conception presupposes that agents who are originators of their own intentional actions are responsible for the effects of their agency. Where responsibility as the corollary of freedom and intentional action is denied, dehumanization has achieved its victory. In view of the self-contradictions of the radical interpretation of freedom, which find their most disturbing expression where humans, in the attempt at being more than human, at appropriating divine freedom, end up by being less then human, one might wonder whether the recognition of this situation is not the starting-point of a new negative natural theology in which awareness of God is sought following the *via negativa* in the experience of the self-contradictions of absolute and unlimited human freedom. But is this the only theological perspective from which this situation can be approached?

IV. God and the Affirmation of Freedom

Thesis 10: The Christian gospel addresses humans in the situation of the perversion of freedom with the promise of the redemption of freedom which restores human freedom as created freedom, destined to find its fulfilment in a communion of love.

It is perhaps one of the most significant and often underestimated features of the Christian gospel that it addresses humans in the situation of the perversion of freedom. The hearer of the gospel is addressed in the situation of the failure of freedom as the attempt at self-constitution, at imitating the absolute freedom of God. The situation of the experience of the self-contradictions of radical freedom is the situation that is expressed in the proclamation of the gospel. This is the point of the often criticized negative anthropology which is in Christian faith the presupposition of gaining access to the promise of a positive anthropology. The glory of humanity can only be accepted as a promise if it is based on the recognition of the misery of attempting to be more than human. The radical character of the proclamation becomes clear where we take seriously that it is first presented as a call to repentance.

Repentance is far more than a preliminary stage in the order of salvation which is quickly superseded by the assurance of grace. Its point is that it requires humans caught in the situation of the failure of self-constituted freedom to identify with this failure, to accept the responsibility that freedom implies and to recognize the consequences of absolute freedom as guilt. The escape into unaccountability is barred. It would deprive the Christian gospel of its relevance in a situation characterized by the self-contradictions of radical freedom if this central element of Christian spirituality were to be sacrificed by well-meaning theologians in a desire to be relevant for a new creation-centred spiritual orientation instead of a fall and redemption-centred spirituality.

The judgement over sin as the perversion of freedom belongs to the heart of the Christian gospel which promises not a mild correction of self-constituted freedom, but its redemption. The redemption of freedom requires recognition of the failure of freedom as self-constitution, because it opens up the liberating insight into the distinction between God and humanity in its most radical form, as the contrast between *homo reus* and *deus iustificans*, between accused humanity and the justifying God which Luther claimed is the central theme of all theology.[20]

However, the Christian gospel is not only a call to repentance, requiring acknowledgement of the failure of freedom as self-constitution and thereby disclosing the human situation as one of absolute dependence on divine grace. It is first and foremost the liberating message of God's justifying grace, the proclamation that God has overcome the self-contradiction of self-constituted freedom and restored the broken relationship with fallen human creatures. As such the Christian gospel is the proclamation of the sovereignty of divine freedom[21] in which God the creator freely remains faithful to the fallen human creatures in spite of their attempt to assume the role of the creator in creation by exercising their freedom as radically creative freedom. In the freely given promise of forgiveness, human agents are distinguished from the consequences of their actions which render the exercise of freedom impossible and are in this way reconstituted as agents. This is the redemption of freedom through the acceptance of divine grace, which in forgiving their sins justifies sinners and in this way

---

[20] The full formula is: *homo reus et perditus et deus iustificans vel salvator*, WA 40/2, 328, 1f.

[21] This sovereignty of divine freedom is most radically expressed in Luther's thesis in *De servo arbitrio* that the *liberum arbitrium* is a divine attribute: '*Sequitur nunc, liberum arbitrium esse plane divinum nomen, nec ulli posse competere quam soli divinae maiestati.*' WA 18, 636, 27-9.

reconstitutes their freedom. Interpreted in this way, the redemption of freedom is liberation from freedom for freedom, from the destructive consequences of absolute self-constitutive freedom and for the exercise of redeemed and created human freedom which is called to find fulfilment in communion with God.

Redeemed freedom is therefore essentially finite, relative freedom, freedom which is dependent on finding its orientation in the disclosure of the truth of the gospel. Just as the gospel of redemption has as its central content the faithfulness of the creator to the fallen human creature, so the redemption of freedom is to be interpreted as the restoration of human freedom as created, as the freedom of creatures whose freedom is not constituted *by* them, but constituted *for* them. Where the attempt to exercise human freedom as absolute infinite freedom is interpreted as resulting in the *dislocation* of the human agent in the relational order of creation, the redemption of freedom should be interpreted as the *relocation* in the relational order of creation of the human agent, whose distinction is the exercise of created freedom in solidarity with all created being.

Redeemed freedom as the restoration of created freedom is in this sense interpreted as freedom which depends for its ground on the relationship to God and which also finds its fulfilment in a communion with God which is not a goal of human action, but a gift of God's grace. Neither the ground nor the ultimate destiny of human freedom lie within the range of human action.

Thesis 11: The notion of an image which is constitutive for the promise of created and redeemed freedom is that of image as transparency *which discloses the relationship to God as the ground, the limitation and the fulfilment of freedom. It finds its archetype and true exemplar in Christ.*

We have so far interpreted central aspects of the Christian gospel as the shattering of the graven image of self-constituted human freedom which is fashioned in the image of God by imitating divine freedom. This raises the question whether there is still room for understanding human freedom as freedom created in the image of God. Can we retain this understanding of the distinction of humans in the order of creation, or is it a casualty of the destructive consequences of interpreting freedom as self-constituted freedom? Beyond salvage, if we follow the direction of the argument, is the thesis of the qualitative identity and quantitative difference which defines human freedom as the imitation and ultimately substitution of divine freedom. The understanding of freedom as redeemed freedom is based on the most decisive difference between human and divine freedom, the difference between humanity accused of the perversion of freedom and the God who justifies sinners. This is the real infinite qualitative difference which informs the interpretation of human freedom as redeemed created freedom.[22]

There is, however, another understanding of the image-relation which interprets the image not as *imitation*, but as *transparency*, where the image cannot replace the reality that is imaged, but remains image only and only insofar as it remains transparent to the reality it depicts. The understanding of image as transparency is based on the radical distinction of the image and the reality it expresses. It is only through this dissimilarity that the similarity between the image and the reality it images can be disclosed. Furthermore, where image is understood as imitation, the imaging relation is established through the activity of the image, and that is the reason why imitation tends to become substitution. When image is understood as transparency, the imaging relation is established by the reality which is disclosed in the transparency of the image. Human being as *imago libertatis* in the sense of transparency which we have described is *established* in what human agents cannot do, but it is *expressed* in what human agents do, in the way they exercise their finite freedom. If we understand human freedom in this sense as the image of divine freedom, then it is the practice of finite freedom which becomes transparent for God's freedom as its infinite ground. Human freedom can become transparent where it rejects the attempt at understanding itself as self-constituted freedom and so discloses divine freedom as its ground, where it denies its capacity for ultimate self-determination and so discloses God's freedom as the destiny of all created being. In the practice of redeemed freedom, human freedom can disclose God's redeeming freedom, and in exercising freedom as created freedom it can become transparent for God's creative freedom.

This freedom as transparency has as its archetype and true exemplar the true image in the humanity of Christ. It is in the

---

[22] Karl Barth who, with Kierkegaard, interpreted in the preface of the second edition of *Romans* the 'infinite qualitative difference' between time and eternity as his 'system', I would maintain that the the real 'infinitive qualitative difference' which we should persistently keep an eye on is the one between sin and grace. This has important implications — not least for the interpretation of the relationship of time and eternity. 'Wenn ich ein "System" habe, so besteht es darin, daß ich das, was Kierkegaard den "unendlichen qualitativen Unterschied" von Zeit und Ewigkeit genannt hat, in seiner negativen und positiven Bedeutung möglichs beharrlich im Auge behalte.' Karl Barth, *Der Römerbrief* (2nd edition, München: Chr. Kaiser Verlag, 1922), p.XII.

image of Christ, where freedom is exercised as rooted in the will of the Father and mediated in the power of the Spirit that the true character of the image of God is disclosed to us, both as the divine freedom for grace and as the human freedom of obedience. For sinners who are justified by the cross of Christ being in the image of God means therefore being conformed to Christ in the power of the Spirit. Christ is therefore both the revelation of the divine freedom of grace and the disclosure of the human freedom of obedience, where obedience to the will of God the Father is not the abrogation of human freedom but the form of its exercise.

Thesis 12: The true measure of freedom is love as the relationship which makes the flourishing of the other the condition of self-fulfilment. Human freedom becomes the icon of divine freedom where the freedom of divine grace constitutes the grace of human freedom.

For Christian faith, it is claimed, most famously by Albrecht Ritschl, the summary concept of God is love.[23] It is significant that it is not claimed that freedom is the complete concept of God. Freedom, as we have seen, requires orientation, requires to be directed towards the achievement of values, towards the establishment and fulfilment of relationship. In itself freedom is the formal capacity for self-determination, for the self-direction of intentional action. This applies to God as well as to humanity. This is the reason why the nominalists qualified the notion of *potentia absoluta* with the concept of *potentia ordinata*. The self-determination of God takes the form of the self-limitation of God which is given in the act of creation and completed in redemption and salvation. Freedom as the formal capacity of self-determination does not imply love. But love presupposes freedom, freedom not to make self-realization the sole ultimate purpose of one's actions, but to choose freely to make the flourishing of the other a necessary condition of self-realization. Perhaps the two notions of divine love and divine freedom can be brought together by saying that in God freedom is the form of love, but love is the content, the *body of freedom*.

Where human beings are conformed to the image of Christ, the true image of God, they are called and enabled to exercise their

---

[23] Albrecht Ritschl, *Unterricht in der christlichen Religion* (Bonn: A. Marcus and E. Weber's Verlag, 1875), p.8: 'Der vollständige christliche Begriff von Gott ist die Liebe.' For a compelling analysis of the model of love and its application to the divine-human relationship cf. Vincent Brümmer, *The Model of Love: A Study in Philosophical Theology* (Cambridge: Cambridge University Press, 1993).

freedom as the freedom of love, as the freedom to make the fulfilment of the other the condition and criterion of self-fulfilment, and in this way become the image of God who is a communion of love. That most poignant image of hope, the Kingdom of God, expresses the relation of free divine love and loving human freedom together in depicting the ultimate purpose of God's action as the perfected community of love with his creation. The fulfilment of God's reign and the salvation of creation are actualized together in the community of the love of God and God's creation. Perhaps it is only at this point, which is anticipated in the images of Christian hope, that *liberté*, *égalité* and *fraternité* will be fully realized together. But if it is true that the coming of the Kingdom has begun in Christ may we not trust that we can already experience anticipatory signs of the full realization of the Kingdom of God in a community of love of free and equal brothers and sisters? Wherever and whenever this happens — or with the tradition: *ubi et quando visum est Deo* — the freedom of divine grace has become the grace of human freedom and we are already what we will be: *imagines libertatis*, images of divine freedom.

6. Christ, Law and Freedom: A Study in Theological Hermeneutics

Francis Watson

It is a fundamental thesis of Pauline theology that Christ has freed us from the law; and it is a fundamental assumption of Pauline interpreters that something of great theological significance is being said here, and that the task of exegesis is to penetrate the surface of the texts in order to discover, concealed in the depths, the reality that here comes to expression. On the surface, however, what is said is simply that the Jewish law is not binding upon Christians. (There is of course an overlap between Jewish and early Christian ethical teaching, but Paul rarely appeals to the law to support an ethical imperative.) Thus, Paul admonishes the Galatians: 'For freedom Christ has set us free; stand fast, therefore, and do not submit again to a yoke of slavery' (Gal 5.1). What does he mean? Simply that his readers are not to submit themselves to circumcision or to the other ordinances of the law which follow from it (Gal 5.2-3, 4.21): for the Galatians have been freed from the enslaving yoke of the law. We might describe this as the 'literal' interpretation of the Pauline thesis that Christ has freed us from the law.

But *why* does Paul assume that Christ and law are mutually exclusive? This question cannot adequately be answered by referring to texts in which the law is presented in a negative light, as the bringer of 'condemnation' (2 Cor 3.9) or a 'curse' (Gal 3.10), for this would merely raise the further question why Paul chooses to define the law in these negative terms. One way to proceed is to remove the limitations imposed by the concretion of the terms 'Christ' and 'law'. As a concrete particularity, 'Christ' refers to the life, death and resurrection of Jesus, who, as the Christ, remains the focal point of a new communal life; and 'law' refers to a series of texts regarded as normative for the practice and beliefs of another, older form of communal life. In order to explain why this 'Christ' and this 'law' exclude one another, it is thought necessary to ask what broader realities underlie the two particularities and are represented by them. 'Law' may be held to represent the broader category of a 'legal' religion in which everyday conduct is subjected to a mass of rules and prohibitions. 'Christ' will then represent the antithesis of this: a religion in which one is freed from legal burdens in order to enter into a personal relationship with God.[1] Or, another way of putting it, 'law' may be said to represent an autonomous human striving to obtain God's favour on the basis of what one is and achieves, in which case 'Christ' will represent the divine acceptance bestowed upon us irrespective of personal qualities and achievements.[2] This might be described as the 'representative' interpretation of the thesis that Christ has freed us from the law, for its interest lies not in the particularity of the entities designated 'Christ' and 'law' but in their power to represent universal, symmetrically-opposed truth-claims about the divine-human relation.

Recent exegesis has made out a strong case for the literal as opposed to the representative interpretation of Paul's claim that Christ has freed us from the law.[3] It is probably true that at some points Paul's texts suggest more universal concerns, in which case the representative interpretation has a genuine exegetical basis to which to appeal. But the literal interpretation does not have to claim

---

[1] On this view, to be justified by faith is to 'enter the world of a gracious God, out of which the old hard legal requirements, with the old hard boundaries of our personality and the old self-regarding claim of rights, have disappeared, a world which is the household of our Father where order and power and ultimate reality are of love and not of law'. John Oman, *Grace and Personality* (Cambridge: Cambridge University Press, 4th edition 1931), p.213.

[2] 'A specifically human striving has merely taken on its culturally and, in point of time, individually distinct form in Judaism. For it is, in fact, a striving common to all men, to gain recognition of one's achievement; and this generates pride.' Christ, as the end of the law, is 'the end of a life which, sustained by the need for recognition (implying secret dread and hatred of God), seeks to establish its own righteousness;... he is the means of access to the way of salvation through grace for the true believer, that is, for the man who gives up his own righteousness and surrenders himself completely to the God who leads man from death into life'. Rudolf Bultmann, *Essays Philosophical and Theological* (ET London: SCM Press, 1955), pp.45, 54.

[3] This approach has been described as 'the new perspective on Paul' – the title of an article by J. D. G. Dunn, *BJRL* 65 (1983), pp.95-122. See my *Paul, Judaism and the Gentiles: A Sociological Approach* (SNTSMS 56, Cambridge: Cambridge University Press, 1986), pp.1-18, for analysis of the contrast between this approach and the 'Lutheran' perspective of Bultmann and many other interpreters of Paul. Works that have helped to establish this 'new perspective' include K. Stendahl, *Paul among Jews and Gentiles* (Philadelphia: Fortress Press, 1976); E. P.

that Paul *never* sees beyond the opposition of two particularities, only that his language is *in the first instance* highly concrete. The following exegetical conclusions are now widely accepted:

(i) In developing his doctrine of freedom from the law, Paul is not engaging in a systematic, general theorizing about the divine-human relationship. His theorizing reflects the concrete historical setting of his mission to the Gentiles.[4]

(ii) As apostle to the Gentiles, Paul established largely Gentile Christian communities in which the Jewish law — most notably the commandments regarding circumcision, the food laws, and the sabbath — was not observed. The doctrine of justification by faith in Christ and not by works of the law implies two different modes of communal life; Paul's denial of the normative status of the law as the code of conduct of the people of God preserves the distinctiveness of his congregations over against the Jewish community.[5]

(iii) For the Jew, observance of the law is a response to the disclosure of the will of God at Sinai. This disclosure does not take

Sanders, *Paul and Palestinian Judaism: A Comparison of Patterns of Religion* (London: SCM Press, 1977); *Paul, the Law and the Jewish People* (Philadelphia: Fortress Press, 1983); H. Räisänen, *Paul and the Law* (Philadelphia: Fortress Press, 1986); *The Torah and Christ: Essays in German and English on the Problem of the Law in Early Christianity* (Helsinki: Finnish Exegetical Society, 1986); *Jesus, Paul and Torah: Collected Essays* (JSNTSupp 43, Sheffield: JSOT Press, 1992); J. M. G. Barclay, *Obeying the Truth: A Study of Paul's Ethics in Galatians* (Edinburgh: T&T Clark, 1988); J. D. G. Dunn, *Romans* (two vols.), Word Biblical Commentary (Dallas: Word Books, 1988); *Jesus, Paul and the Law* (London: SPCK, 1990); J. A. Ziesler, *Paul's Letter to the Romans* (London: SCM Press, 1989).

4   The fact that Paul's thinking derives from his experience as a missionary does not mean that he cannot be regarded as a theologian (the view of Räisänen, *Paul and the Law*, p.267). 'Paul's qualification to be called a "theologian" is not ... that he wrote "systematic theology". Obviously he did not. His qualification lies in the way he went about obeying his vocation. His sense of purpose, call and mission demand to be understood in terms of a worldview which can only be called "theological".' N. T. Wright, *The Climax of the Covenant: Christ and the Law in Pauline Theology* (Edinburgh: T&T Clark, 1991, p.262).

5   This contrast between two distinct forms of communal life would have to be restated if Sanders is right to claim that the law is excluded only as a requirement of entry into the Christian community but that as a code governing behaviour it is retained — with the exception of some of its more distinctively Jewish elements. *Paul, the Law and the Jewish People*, pp.113-14. But this is an unsatisfactory distinction: for if the law is to be fulfilled within the Christian community, then it is a requirement of entry that one accept the obligation to obey the law. It

the form of sheer demand, but is subsequent to the divine election of Israel through the patriarchs and to the deliverance from Egypt. God's covenantal obligations precede and ground the corresponding human obligations. Paul himself acknowledges the context of 'works of the law' within the Jewish theology of the covenant.[6]

(iv) Paul opposes the circumcision of his Gentile converts because circumcision is the rite of entry into the Jewish people, and not because it is an example of a 'good work' which helps to establish merit.[7] Thus in Galatians the issue between Paul and his opponents is not whether and how far one must perform good works in order to be saved, but the conditions for membership of the people of God.[8]

(v) If the opposition of 'faith' to 'works' refers in the first instance to the distinction between the Christian and the Jewish communities, then this opposition is compatible with passages which assert that a reorientation of conduct in response to the gospel is indispensable for salvation.[9] This reorientation can only occur within an ecclesial context.

It is assumed on both sides in the exegetical debate that an emphasis on particularities is characteristic of a primarily 'historical' orientation, whereas a 'theological' orientation will wish to emphasize the representative function of the particularities. Either the text is studied as a historical document deriving from a context which is quite different from our own; or its contemporary

would be preferable to distinguish between, on the one hand, references to the law as the scriptural code governing the life of the Jewish community, and, on the other hand, the occasional appeal to specific commandments which conform to Christian ethical requirements (cf. Gal 5.14, Rom 8.4, 13.8-10).

6   Sanders' criticism of the pejorative view of Judaism as a religion of legalistic works-righteousness is well-known; see his *Paul and Palestinian Judaism*, especially pp.33-59. Sanders argues that the expression 'covenantal nomism' does more justice to the character of Palestinian Judaism (pp.419-28), and can cite Paul as a witness to this. *Paul, the Law and the Jewish People*, p.46.

7   This point is made, in opposition to Bultmann, in my *Paul, Judaism and the Gentiles*, p.69. One corollary of this is that 'if it was no longer circumcision but baptism which was the primary rite of initiation, then women became full members of the people of God with the same rights and duties'. E. Schüssler Fiorenza, *In Memory of Her: A Feminist Theological Reconstruction of Christian Origins* (London: SCM Press, 1983), p.210.

8   So Stendahl, *Paul among Jews and Gentiles*, p.2.

9   Cf. Sanders, *Paul, the Law and the Jewish People*, pp.105-6.

theological relevance is asserted on the basis of its representative possibilities. The question whether non-Jewish Christians should submit to the Jewish law was once of vital concern, but it is so no longer — unless it can be shown that something more fundamental and more general is at stake here than what appears on the surface. Yet the assumption that particularities are as such theologically uninteresting is obviously problematic. The assumption might be justified if we knew in advance that Christian faith is concerned with the necessary truths of reason rather than the contingent truths of history; a rationalist hermeneutic along these lines would dissolve all contingencies into generalities in its attempt to establish a 'religion within the limits of reason alone'. But Christian faith has tended to believe that certain contingencies are supremely important. It is of course not the case that every particularity referred to in the New Testament is theologically significant, but it is at least worth asking whether the Pauline thesis that Christ frees us from the law might be theologically significant precisely in its particularity and not in spite of it.[10]

I. The Prejudice against Particularity

The tension between representative and literal interpretations of Paul's doctrine of freedom from the law is not a purely modern one, but stems from the unprecedented importance Luther assigned to this doctrine by installing it at the centre of his reordering of Christian faith. It will be instructive to trace in Luther's position the antecedents of the modern hermeneutical assumptions I have outlined.

What does Paul mean when he asserts that Christ has set us free (Gal 5.1)? In his commentary on Galatians of 1535, Luther argues that 'Christ has set us free, not for a political freedom or a freedom of the flesh but for a theological or spiritual freedom, that is, to make our conscience free and joyful, unafraid of the wrath to

---

[10]   The hermeneutical and theological significance of the literal sense in its irreducible particularity is emphasized especially by Hans Frei; see his *The Eclipse of Biblical Narrative: A Study in Eighteenth and Nineteenth Century Hermeneutics* (New Haven and London: Yale University Press, 1974); *The Identity of Jesus Christ: The Hermeneutical Bases of Dogmatic Theology* (Philadelphia: Fortress Press, 1975); G. Hunsinger and W. C. Placher (eds), *Types of Christian Theology* (New Haven and London: Yale University Press, 1992). On Frei, see my *Text, Church and World: Biblical Interpretation in Theological Perspective* (Edinburgh: T&T Clark, 1994), ch.1.

come.'[11] Yet in this text Paul speaks not of freedom in general but of freedom from the yoke of slavery, and in the following verse he appears to identify that yoke not with terror of the wrath of God but with circumcision: 'Now I, Paul, say to you that if you receive circumcision Christ will be of no advantage to you.' The explanation is that 'Paul is not discussing the actual deed in and of itself, which has nothing wrong in it if there is no trust in it or presumption of righteousness; but he is discussing how the deed is used, namely, the trust and the righteousness that are attached to the deed.'[12] The reference to 'circumcision' is stripped of its particularity — any other pious deed might have been referred to — and interpreted as representing the general disposition that often comes to expression through such pious deeds: the disposition to trust that by one's performance of such deeds one acquires righteousness before God. To trust in one's own righteousness is to expose oneself to the wrath of God, and in being freed from the law and the self-righteousness it generates the conscience becomes joyful and fearless. For Luther, it is essential that 'circumcision' should be able to represent not only 'ceremonial' but also 'moral' works. Although

> it is easier to recognize a false reliance on righteousness in ceremonial works than it is in the moral works of the Decalogue, [yet] righteousness must not be sought through these works either; it must be sought through faith in Christ. I am mentioning this lest someone get the impression from what I am saying that the apostle is opposing only the ceremonial features of the Law.[13]

Thus, the thesis that Christ frees us from the law means that Christ frees us from the attempt to attain righteousness before God by performing the actions that the law requires, whether ceremonial or moral. Luther must presuppose the capacity of 'circumcision' to represent moral as well as (Christian) ceremonial deeds oriented towards righteousness, if the promise of freedom from the law is to remain existentially relevant for his hearers and readers. If it represented only the 'ceremonial' deeds distinctive of Judaism, it would have a merely historical interest for them. Justification by faith in Christ and not by works of the law would then mean simply that it is we Christians who are righteous before God, rather than Jews: a point that it was necessary to emphasize

---

[11] *Luther's Works [LW]* (ET Philadelphia: Fortress Press; St Louis: Concordia, 1955-, vol.27), p.4.
[12] *LW* 27.10.
[13] *LW* 27.327.

in the early days of the church but which Luther's contemporaries simply take for granted. If the Pauline gospel is to have any force, it must apply directly to us, announcing *our* freedom from the false disposition underlying our own ethical and ecclesial practices.

Luther is well aware that exegetes have traditionally confined Paul's polemic against works of the law to distinctively Jewish 'ceremonies'; and, in his view, it is impossible to exaggerate the significance of this fundamental exegetical error, for which Jerome is largely to blame. Opposition to Jerome on this point is already signalled in the 1519 commentary on Galatians. With reference to Gal 3.2: 'Did you receive the Spirit by works of the law, or by hearing with faith?', Luther writes:

> I surely do not believe it when in this passage St Jerome distinguishes the works of the law from good works and thinks that Cornelius received the Spirit on the basis of works; for it is clear that the Holy Spirit descended on them at Peter's preaching, that is, when they heard with faith, as he says here ... The apostle is referring not only to the ceremonial law but to absolutely every law; for since it is faith alone that justifies and does good works, it follows that absolutely no works of any law whatever justify, and that the works of no law are good, but that only the works of faith are good.[14]

Jerome cites the example of Cornelius (cf. Acts 10.2, 35) to prove that the faith with which the Spirit is received is not without 'good works', the pattern of behaviour approved by God; thus the 'works of the law' that are *contrasted* with 'faith' must refer only to Jewish ceremonies. Luther rejects this restriction, and his whole doctrine of justification hangs on this point.

In the *de Servo Arbitrio* of 1525, the opposition to Jerome is still more emphatic. The claim that 'works of the law' refers only to Jewish ceremonies incompatible with Christian faith is, Luther tells us,

> the ignorant error of Jerome, which, in spite of Augustine's strenuous resistance, — God having withdrawn and let Satan prevail — has spread out into the world and has persisted to the present day. It has consequently become impossible to understand Paul, and the knowledge of Christ has been inevitably obscured. Even if there had never been any other error in the church, this one alone was pestilent and potent enough to make havoc of the gospel.[15]

Jerome's narrowing of the scope of 'works' prevailed over Augustine's comprehensive view, and this is the fundamental apostasy

14   *LW* 27.247, 248.
15   *LW* 33.258.

of church history. Jerome's original sin, like Adam's, is inspired by Satan and infects generation after generation of his theological descendants. A mistake over this one word has proved sufficiently disastrous to make the true Pauline gospel unintelligible for centuries. As Christ comes to reverse the effects of Adam's fall, so Luther comes to reverse the effects of Jerome's misreading; church history re-enacts the history of the world's salvation.

The 'misreading' of Galatians or Romans will depict the apostle as engaging in controversy with Judaism or Jewish Christianity. He is convinced — rightly, as later Christian orthodoxy believes — that Christ has abolished the ceremonies of the Jewish law. The opposition of 'faith in Christ' to 'works of the law' is therefore an appeal to Jews and Jewish Christians not to insist on the continuing necessity of those ceremonies, and to Gentile Christians to resist those who seek to impose ceremonies on them. Christ is the divinely-appointed way to salvation, not Judaism. Thus Jerome represents an embryonic 'literal-historical' reading of Paul, sensitive to the particularities to which the apostle addresses himself. Luther's assumption is that this concern with first-century particularities conceals the crucially-important theological claims of the texts. Jerome's view is still concerned with theological truth: the truth that Jesus Christ does not require us to submit to the Jewish law. But for Luther it is only insofar as the conscience hears itself addressed by the judging and comforting word of God that one can speak of theological truth. A truth that exists outside of the conscience in the world of objective history is at best a piece of scaffolding, radically subordinate to the encounter in which I hear myself addressed by the word of God. If this word is to be based in holy scripture, then it is necessary that the scriptural word should relate to our ultimate concern and not merely to past contingencies.

Operating here, it seems, is a kind of *prejudice against historical particularity*; the assumption that the historically particular is in itself theologically irrelevant, only becoming theologically relevant insofar as it represents the general and ultimate concern of the conscience here and now.[16] True theological signifi-

---

[16] Compare Kant's hermeneutic, in which the prejudice against particularity takes a more extreme form: 'It is possible to explain how an historical account is to be put to a moral use without deciding whether this is the intention of the author or merely our interpretation, provided this meaning is true in itself, apart from all historical proof, and is moreover the only way in which we can derive something conducive to our betterment from a passage which otherwise would be only an unfruitful addition to our historical knowledge', Immanuel Kant, *Religion within the Limits of Reason Alone* [1793] (ET New York: Harper and Row, 1960).

cance is not to be found *within* the literal-historical sense of a text, but only *beyond* it. Whatever space is conceded to the literal-historical sense, the orientation will always be away from the merely particular towards the universal and ultimate concerns of the conscience. In an article entitled 'Reflections on the Doctrine of the Law' (1958), Gerhard Ebeling notes that in Luther 'the concepts law and gospel are largely stripped of the concrete historical references they bear in Paul and made into hard-and-fast general basic concepts of theology, so that they find a more universal application than in Paul'.[17] We must proceed more cautiously, for 'certain essential elements in the Pauline concept of *nomos* appear to oppose the extension of the concept of law which takes place in the theology of the Reformers.'[18] Despite this concession, however, the way from particular to universal can claim some support from the Pauline texts. For example, Romans and 1 Corinthians suggest a concern with the problem of the law even among Gentile readers: 'Paul obviously did not merely expect the Gentiles to be interested in the problem of the Jewish law, but apparently also believed that they would discover in these discussions of it something which directly concerned themselves.'[19] On the one hand, Paul's texts refer to historical particularities; on the other hand, they imply that those particularities represent realities which are theologically relevant to those who are not concerned about the church's relation to Judaism. Theological relevance occurs not in historical particularity but in spite of it.

These exegetical claims serve to justify an existentalist interpretation of the Pauline language, a characteristic example of which is given in a later work dating from 1981, where Ebeling interprets Paul's faith/works antithesis as follows:

> What matters is what I live by, what I rely upon, what I take as the ground of my existence, what I understand to be my purpose with respect to God: is it faith, and therefore God himself in his grace, or is it my own demonstrable reality, and therefore I myself in what I achieve and represent?[20]

'Works' here represents not the practice of Judaism but a life based on my own status and achievements in the sphere of everyday reality; a representative, non-literal interpretation very similar to Luther's, despite the difference of idiom, and equally opposed to any attempt to find theological significance in the

[17] G. Ebeling, *Word and Faith* (ET London: SCM Press, 1963), p.261.
[18] Ebeling, *Word and Faith*, p.275.
[19] Ebeling, *Word and Faith*, p.274.
[20] G. Ebeling, *The Truth of the Gospel: An Exposition of Galatians* (ET Philadelphia: Fortress Press, 1985), pp.176-7.

obvious primary reference to the practice of Judaism. Christ frees us from the law, but the reference to the concrete practice of Judaism has been supplanted by a reflection on a general human orientation from which we are freed by the word of the gospel.

Who is the 'I' who is addressed by the divine word in the gospel? On Ebeling's view, the 'I' is the person who is disposed to live on the basis of a demonstrable, empirical, social reality in which he or she occupies a certain position and fulfils certain roles; the word of the gospel exposes the questionableness of this attempt at an autonomous existence, disclosing that the only true ground of our existence is God himself. In this account, the gospel radically individualizes the socialized self, momentarily isolating it from the complex networks of fallen relationships in which it is entangled and confronting it with the foundational reality of an I-Thou relationship with the creator. It is held that the biblical texts are to be interpreted in such a way that their witness to this fundamental encounter is clear, in conformity with their appointed role as the vehicle of this encounter. Interpretation cannot itself bring about this event, but it can try to ensure that understanding conforms to faith.

All this may well be open to criticism on theological grounds. As interpretation of Pauline language, however, Ebeling's comments should not be too quickly rejected.[21] Unlike Luther, Ebeling is aware that the move from the particular to the universal will involve some loss of focus. An 'existentialist' interpretation will not try to maintain the close adherence to the letter of the text that is appropriate to a more 'literal' interpretation, for their purposes are different: on the one hand, to draw out theological implications that transcend particularity, on the other hand, to render the individual text with the greatest possible clarity and precision. At a certain level of abstraction, it is true that, in antithesis to 'faith', the term 'works' can stand for 'my own demonstrable reality', 'I myself in what I achieve and represent'. Even at the literal level, 'faith' for Paul is indeed a response called forth by God's grace in Christ, and it is therefore bound far more closely to prevenient divine action than are the (Jewish) 'works', which allow correspondingly greater scope for semi-autonomous human action. The theological claim that we are justified by God's grace and not by our own actions remains

---

[21] Works in the 'new perspective' vein (including my own) are too ready to accuse the previous exegetical tradition of 'imposing anachronistic Lutheran categories onto Paul' — as though the removal of later accretions would result in an unproblematic, purely historical Paul who has nothing at all in common with Luther. The actual hermeneutical situation is more complex.

firmly grounded in the Pauline texts. Even the literal sense of the
text may sometimes hint at implications transcending the particular issue under discussion, and it would be wrong to forbid attempts
to follow up those implications. A hermeneutic that rejected every
kind of distinction between what is said and what is meant would
soon prove rigid and oppressive.

On the other hand, where an interpretative tradition has long
concealed or overlooked particularity in its concern for the universal,
an emphasis on particularity may be necessary in order to redress the
balance. An interpretation oriented towards the universal inevitably
reorders and unbalances the complex of interrelated particulars that
constitutes the surface of the text, assigning theological potential to
some while relegating others to the margins. Literal-historical interpretation can be of theological value in restoring the original interre-
latedness and thereby enabling quite different kinds of theological
exploration. On the basis of recent literal-historical interpretation, I
shall argue that the Pauline theme of freedom from the law has to do
with the laying of permanent foundations for subsequent Christian
communal identity.

II. The Elements of Christian Grammar

Recent exegesis of Galatians and Romans has achieved a certain
clarity of focus in emphasizing the extent to which Paul's thinking
is dominated by the ecclesial question of the relationship between
Jews and Gentiles. However, it has largely failed to develop its
insights in a theological direction, with the result that an interpretation along the lines laid down by Luther still seems compelling
if it is theological engagement rather than historical clarification
that one is seeking.[22] The question is therefore whether a literal-
historical reading is capable of serving as the basis for a theological interpretation of these texts.

Why is it often assumed that the modern literal-historical
interpretation of the Pauline theme of freedom from the law is of
little direct theological value? The effect of this interpretation, it
is said, is to show the extent to which Paul's theological horizons
are dominated by a first-century issue that is irrelevant to 'our
own concerns' — meaning, perhaps, issues of social justice, or the

---

[22] Thus John Ziesler argues that the 'new perspective' is exegetically
justified but that Luther's interpretation is still appropriate theologically, if it is regarded as exposition rather than exegesis, 'Justification
by Faith in the Light of the "New Perspective" on Paul', *Theology* 94
(1991), pp.188-94.

need for radical reinterpretation of Christian beliefs, or the quest for ecumenical and inter-faith understanding, or opposition to fundamentalism.[23] A biblical text will be 'relevant' when it says something that can be placed at the disposal of one or other of these concerns of ours. According to this hermeneutic, many texts fail to meet our criterion of relevance, and integrity demands that they be left outside the informal canon within the canon established by the way we construe our own concerns. The rejected alternative against which this approach defines itself is the claim that every part of the Bible is relevant to us, that its concerns must dictate and determine our concerns, and that what it says is to be directly identified with what God says. If one rejects a biblicism of this kind, one is bound to accept that the theological significance of some parts of the Bible may not be readily apparent. Yet it would be strange if this applied to texts at the heart of the Pauline corpus, considering their immense and varied impact on the subsequent history of Christian theology. No doubt classic texts can and do 'die', losing their ability to speak to the present and thus their classic status. But is the announcement of the death of these particular classics premature?

On the literal-historical reading, it is said, the texts are irrelevant to our own concerns; we become aware of a gulf separating our own world from their first-century world. These hermeneutical claims originate in a purely synchronic criterion of relevance which construes 'our own time' as an autonomous, self-contained sphere out of which certain 'concerns' arise bearing with them a normative claim to exclusive attention.[24] It is not simply that we *choose* to adopt one contemporary concern or another; for these concerns are normative, imposing themselves upon us and demanding the right to reorder our interpretative priorities. It is implied that to refuse such a reordering is to be morally culpable as well as intellectually deficient.

Is there an alternative construal of 'our own concerns' to the impoverished and authoritarian model offered by this cultural

---

[23] The notion of 'relevance to our own concerns', as discussed here, implies the possibility of a *positive* theological evaluation of a text. It is of course possible for a text to be highly 'relevant' for *negative* reasons; thus, Elisabeth Schüssler Fiorenza advocates a mode of biblical interpretation which seeks 'to critically comprehend how the Bible functions in the oppression of women or the poor and thus to prevent its misuse for further oppression', *Bread not Stone: The Challenge of Feminist Biblical Interpretation* (Edinburgh: T&T Clark, 1990), p.57.

[24] For an example of this, see Sallie McFague, *Models of God: Theology for an Ecological, Nuclear Age* (London: SCM Press, 1987), pp.3-6.

relativism? To be concerned about the theological significance of biblical texts is to locate oneself within a communal context which predisposes one to believe that the texts do actually possess such a significance — to a greater or lesser extent, in some way or other. This expectation of theological significance does not have to look for a fortuitous hermeneutical miracle in which the empty letter of the text is suddenly transformed into living address through the spontaneous activity of the Spirit. The expectation of theological significance in the present and the future derives from the fact that Christian communal identity has already been shaped and reshaped by precisely these texts, and from the conviction that no breach in tradition has occurred that is sufficiently serious to prevent their continuing to fulfil this role in the future.[25] We do not possess the texts in the form of bare words on a page, but only as transmitted through the medium of an ongoing tradition, a *Wirkungsgeschichte* in which we too participate and which counterbalances our synchronic relation to our own limited time and place with a diachronic relation to a historic community of faith. If that is the case, then the criterion of relevance to our own concerns will have to be extended: for 'our own concerns' include not only the normative demands of our own time and place but also the concerns that are integral to the diachronic life of the Christian community, which are our concerns too insofar as we participate in that communal life.

These concerns that are integral to the Christian community are, in large part, concerns about communal *identity*. What is the Christian church, and what is it for? By what criteria are claims to be the Christian church assessed? How is the need for identity to *adapt* to changing circumstances compatible with the need for identity to be *preserved* if it is not simply to be lost and replaced with a new identity? Is there a relative stability of communal identity to which we must conform? Or is communal identity what each succeeding generation declares it to be, so that any attempt to assess the church's faithfulness to its own fundamental identity is ruled out? Questions such as these arise out of the entire range of activities in which the Christian church is engaged, from its preaching and sacramental life to the manner of its socio-political

---

[25] This emphasis on an expectation grounded in tradition is broadly compatible with the 'functionalist' understanding of scripture advocated by David Kelsey, who argues that 'to call a set of texts "scripture" is to say that it ought to be used in certain ways in the church's common life so as to nurture and preserve her communal self-identity', *The Uses of Scripture in Modern Theology* (London: SCM Press, 1975), p.147. But to call a set of texts 'scripture' is to see in them the *foundations* of communal identity, and not just a prescribed 'use'.

involvements. Among other things, they enquire about the *language* that is to be employed in the maintenance and development of communal identity and self-definition.[26]

In the Pauline texts, too, we find a preoccupation with the maintenance and development of communal identity; modern literal-historical reading has served to highlight the irreducibly communal and ecclesial nature of these texts' fundamental concerns. But these texts do not merely offer interesting analogies or historical precedents to contemporary struggles over ecclesial self-definition. These are *canonical* texts that have already proved their effectiveness in determining some, if not all, of the directions in which communal identity subsequently developed. In accepting certain of the positions argued in the Pauline texts, the Christian community definitively excluded certain possibilities of self-definition and gave canonical status to others. *Decisions taken by Paul and the early church remain foundational to the identity of the Christian community, and insofar as this is the case Paul's texts cannot be regarded as irrelevant.* There is no yawning historical gulf separating these texts from our own present; the 'gulf' is filled with the tradition which these texts helped to generate and within which they continued to fulfil certain essential roles in the maintenance and development of Christian identity.[27]

It is not necessary to ascribe to an individual canonical text a distinctive role in the establishing of Christian communal identity. In general it will not be possible to distinguish elements of communal identity that derive from one text rather than another; what is important is that all canonical texts participate in one way or another in the establishing of communal identity. There is also a circularity about this process: it may be precisely because communal identity is taking one direction rather than another that a particular text comes to be accepted as canonical. With these provisos in mind, the significance of this analysis for theological interpretation can be further explored by taking Paul's letter to the Galatians as a test-case.

---

26 Communal identity is not produced and maintained only by way of narratives, and it is therefore misleading to speak of 'the narrative identity of the Christian community', G. W. Stroup, *The Promise of Narrative Theology* (London: SCM Press, 1984), p.170.

27 'The important thing is to recognise the distance in time as a positive and productive possibility of understanding. It is not a yawning abyss, but is filled with the continuity of custom and tradition, in the light of which all that is handed down presents itself to us', H.-G. Gadamer, *Truth and Method* (ET London: Sheed and Ward, 2nd edition 1979), pp.264-5.

In Galatians 5.1 it is said: 'For freedom Christ has set us free; stand fast therefore, and do not submit again to a yoke of slavery.' The context is not a debate with another religion (i.e. Judaism) but an inner-Christian debate about Christian identity; the question at issue is whether we have to be or become Jews in order to be Christians. Paul answers this question with an emphatic negative: for a Gentile Christian to adopt the Jewish way of life as defined in the Torah would be to submit to 'a yoke of slavery'. It is not that this can be shown to be the case by empirical demonstration, by appealing for example to the burdens that the law might be thought to impose upon the conscience; this negative assessment of the law appeals instead to a complex allegory in which the slave-girl Hagar represents the law (4.21-31), and to an identification of the law (or the angelic authors of the law?) with the enslaving elemental spirits of the universe (4.1-10).

As arguments, subsequent tradition has not judged these claims to be especially compelling. The assessment of the law is too negative, and does not give enough emphasis to the fact that the traditions relating to Mount Sinai bear witness to an authentic moment of divine disclosure. As regards allegory, the usefulness of this interpretative device for establishing doctrinal conclusions has rightly been questioned. And yet the fundamental thesis, that Christ has set us free from the yoke of the law, has nevertheless been accepted; the inadequacies of the supporting arguments challenge Christian theology to find better arguments (including arguments that try to do justice to the greatness of Judaism), but the conclusion itself is rapidly established in most areas as a fundamental component of subsequent Christian identity. In general, Christians do not submit to circumcision, dietary laws, sabbaths or feasts, despite the fact that these observances are enjoined in texts that they too hold to be authoritative. It proves to be a complex balancing act to maintain the God-given authority of Jewish scripture while denying the normative character of many of its most characteristic ordinances. But, whatever the difficulties, it is soon clear that this particular balancing act is necessary, for it is established as a basic grammatical rule for Christian discourse that Christ has freed us from the yoke of the law.[28]

---

[28] For the interpretation of doctrines as grammatical rules, see G. A. Lindbeck, *The Nature of Doctrine: Religion and Theology in a Postliberal Age* (London: SPCK, 1984), pp.79-82. However, use of this rule-model of doctrine need not entail the conclusion that 'doctrines qua doctrines are not first-order propositions' (p.80), since it is possible to maintain *both* that doctrines are first-order propositions *and* that they also function as grammatical rules for Christian discourse. 'Grammatical rule' is in this context a *metaphor*, which should not be pressed beyond its proper application.

In the establishing of this rule, Paul's opponents' account of Christian identity is rejected. According to this alternative account, Jesus is the Messiah sent to fulfil the divine promises made through the prophets, and the question is who the people are for whom Jesus accomplishes his saving work. Clearly they are people who believe in him; those who disbelieve cut themselves off from God's saving action and are in danger of excluding themselves from his people. But is belief enough? Why should it be thought that Jesus does away with Moses, as though the two were enemies rather than fellow-servants of God? There is, indeed, much in the Law of Moses that seems strange to Gentile enquirers. But in the last resort, it should be enough that God has commanded certain actions and prohibited others; our calling is not to fathom the depths of his wisdom, but to obey — as Jesus did, setting an example of faithfulness to the divine will that his followers of both Jewish and Gentile origin must imitate. For this reason, God raised him from the dead, as he will raise us if we reject ungodly passions and take upon ourselves the gentle yoke of the Torah.

Some such position as this appears to have been asserted as an appropriate foundation for Christian identity, over against the Pauline view. It can appeal more persuasively to scriptural warrants than can Paul, for it accepts the common-sense principle that 'scriptural authority' means that clear, explicit divine commandments remain normative for present-day practice. Its claim that what is said about Jesus should not conflict with what is said about Moses might also seem to have the potential to become a normative rule of Christian grammar. Of course, this position is in fact 'inadequate' as a foundation for Christian identity. But how do we know this to be the case, despite the strong counter-arguments to which the Pauline view seems vulnerable? We know this because we live in the aftermath of the fact that Paul's account was accepted while his opponents' account was rejected. That is not to say that we must trace our communal identity back to an arbitrary decision which has perhaps distorted the truth of its subject-matter. On the contrary, our communal identity rests on the presupposition that the decision in favour of the Pauline view and against his opponents represents a true discernment of the significance of Jesus Christ (although there are no neutral, uncontested criteria available that would enable us to get behind the texts to check which view conforms most closely to the truth.)

Yet our communal identity is not *bound* by the decisions of the early church, which in some cases we revise on the assumption that communal identity must develop and is not a mere given; and so it is possible in principle to imagine that the decision to set Christian communal identity at a distance from Jewish communal identity could be reversed. One cannot rule out *a priori* the legitimacy of advocating some such reversal or revision. So far, however, it has been such a fundamental component of Christian communal identity to maintain its distinctiveness over against Judaism that it is hard to see how it could be surrendered without at the same time losing the basic truth-claim that God was in Christ reconciling the world to himself. The view that Christian distinctiveness over against Judaism is inherently anti-Semitic, and that the Christian community is therefore morally obligated to abandon or diminish this distinctiveness, overlooks the possibility that conflicting truth-claims may be fully compatible with ethical responsibility towards the other.[29]

Freedom from the yoke of the Law of Moses has as its positive corollary a view of Jesus Christ as the ultimate and universal form of divine self-disclosure. The terms 'ultimacy' and 'universality' refer to truth-claims about Jesus Christ which are at the same time grammatical rules of Christian discourse. He is 'ultimate' in the sense that the narrative of God's self-disclosure to his people Israel reaches its climax and its conclusion in him. Although history and divine self-disclosure continue, this ongoing divine self-disclosure occurs through the mediation of the community, texts and sacraments which bear witness to Jesus Christ, so that a supplementary narrative of further divine self-disclosure is ruled out. His significance is 'universal' in the sense that the hermeneutical horizon within which he is to be located is not the Jewish community whose Messiah he is, but the world, into which he enters as God's incarnate Son (cf. Gal 4.1-5). As a rule of Christian discourse, the truth-claim that his significance is 'uni-

---

[29] I have in mind here anti-Christian statements such as the following: 'The roots of Christian antisemitism need be traced no further than Christianity itself; Christians have been antisemitic because they have been Christians ... We must learn, I think, to live with the unpleasant fact that antisemitism is part of what it has meant historically to be a Christian, and is still part of what it means to be Christian', R. L. Wilken, *The Myth of Christian Beginnings: History's Impact on Belief* (New York: Doubleday, 1972), p.197. Or this: 'How is it possible to construe and proclaim the resurrection of Jesus other than in supersessionist and triumphalist ways? ... For is it not God who through a special sacred-historical act vindicates the Christian faith in the face of its denial by Jews? ... Are we driven to conclude, then, that at its very center the Christian faith is deprived, or acts to deprive itself, of moral credibility?', A. R. Eckardt, 'Salient Christian-Jewish Issues of Today: A Christian Exploration', in J. H. Charlesworth (ed.), *Jews and Christians: Exploring the Past, Present, and Future* (New York: Crossroad, 1990), pp.150-77; pp.162-3.

versal' excludes the possible claim that independent, equally-
valid divine self-disclosures must occur elsewhere in the world,
since Jesus Christ is too culture-bound and limited a symbol to be
more than merely local in his significance. The basic grammatical
rules of Christian discourse that refer us to Jesus' ultimacy and
universality are already implicit in Paul's text, which sees in his
opponents' proclamation a threat to that ultimacy and universality.[30]

The ongoing effect of this decision by Paul and the early
Christian community can be seen in the basic shape of the
Christian canon, which is far more than a mere list of authoritative books divided into two collections.[31] In the Jewish canon,
however unclear its boundaries may still have been, the undis-
puted centre is occupied by the five books that constitute the Law
of Moses; the rest is necessary supplementation, elaboration and
commentary. The Christian canon might have been closely modelled on this Jewish paradigm, in which case Christian and Jewish
communal identities would have remained in close proximity to
one another. There do not appear to be any necessary limits to the
canonical process in which the Law of Moses is supplemented by
additional books; an increasing number of supplementary books
need not pose a threat to the centrality of the Law. Thus, distinctively Christian books (including Gospels and letters) could have
been added as a fourth element to the existing threefold canon
comprising law, prophets and writings, in such a way that the
primacy of the law was maintained. Had Paul's opponents' account of Christian identity been accepted, a canonical structuring
of this kind would have been a logical consequence.

On the other hand, Paul's assumption of the ultimate and
universal significance of Jesus Christ has as its logical conse-

---

[30] This reading would be disputed by Sidney G. Hall III, who claims that
'Paul equips Gentiles with a christology that allows Christians — the
modern-day heirs of the Gentiles — to experience Christ as their
decisive re-presentation of God's love, while also allowing Jews, with
different faith communities, to experience righteousness through
other decisive re-presentations of God's love', *Christian anti-Semitism
and Paul's Theology* (Philadelphia: Fortress Press, 1993), p.133. The
obvious implausibility of this interpretation of Paul should not detract
from the more important issue of whether a 'Christology after Auschwitz'
(p.133) is really obliged to take this general form.

[31] James Barr's attempt to confine the meaning of 'canon' to 'list' is
unconvincing, *Holy Scripture: Canon, Authority and Criticism* (Oxford: Oxford University Press, 1983), p.49. The Christian 'Old Testament' may contain exactly the same books as the holy scripture of the
Jewish community, but yet be a very different entity.

quence a rejection of the foundational status of the Law of Moses
and its replacement by Jesus Christ as the centre of the Christian
canon. Thus the 'New Testament' is not a fourth element added to
the threefold Jewish canon founded on the Torah but a new
foundation that entails a radical restructuring of the Jewish canon
so that it becomes a new, unheard-of entity, the Christian 'Old
Testament'. This canonical restructuring is foundational for Christian identity; it is difficult to imagine how the decision could be
reversed, so that the Gospels were reduced in status to secondary
elaborations of the Torah, because it is difficult to imagine how
such a revision could possibly be regarded within the Christian
community as adequate to the ultimacy and universality of the
truth-claim it hears within the Gospels. Paul's decision partici-
pates in a canonical process whose effects have proved to be
enduring.

The existence of a Christian 'Old Testament' is arguably as
fundamental to Christian identity as the existence of a 'New
Testament'. (How can a 'testament' or covenant be described as
'new' if not in relation to another that is 'old'?) Here too the
theological decisions that Paul takes in writing to the Galatians
participate in the establishing of basic rules of Christian discourse. Again, a possible alternative account of Christian identity
is definitively excluded: an account in which the Jewish scriptures
are handed back to the Jews, so that Christians are left with a
canon consisting solely of Christian writings. Why should Paul not
have taken his dichotomy between Moses and Christ to what
might seem its logical (proto-Marcionite) conclusion, a denial of
the normative status of the Jewish scriptures within the Christian
community? Would this have made his argument for the sole
authority of Jesus Christ more persuasive for his readers? Do his
apparent equivocations about the divine origin of the law (Gal.
3.15-20, 4.1-10) indicate that he was tempted to take this route?

Be that as it may, Paul in fact rejected the possibility of
excluding Jewish scripture from any role in the creation of Christian communal identity; and he rejected this possibility as deci-
sively as he rejected the opposite possibility of conceding to Jewish
scripture the role of *determining* Christian communal identity.
Jewish scripture does not control the interpretation of Jesus
Christ; on the contrary, scripture is reinterpreted from the standpoint of a Jesus Christ to whom ultimate and universal significance is ascribed. In this light, the potential universality of the
promises to Abraham is highlighted (Gal 3.6-9, 15-18, 29), the
exodus is passed over without comment despite the language of
slavery and freedom, the non-narrative parts of the Pentateuch
are drastically subordinated (3.12, 19-25), and the prophets become witnesses to Christ rather than commentators on the Torah

(3.11, 4.27). The details of this fundamental restructuring of Jewish scripture did not necessarily prove convincing: even Paul abandons in Romans 4 the claim of Galatians 3.16 that 'Abraham's seed' refers to 'Christ'.

Far more important than the cogency of the details, however, is to note the magnitude of what is here undertaken: the beginning of a restructuring of Jewish scripture which will lead to the creation of a new entity, the Christian 'Old Testament', whose outlines are already discernible here in embryonic form. Once again, it is the fundamental shape of subsequent Christian communal identity that is here being determined (although the historic role of these arguments becomes clear only in retrospect). A reversal or revision of the Pauline and early Christian decision here is, indeed, an imaginable possibility; the Christian community might come to accept the claim that the Christian 'Old Testament' represents an illegitimate and violent seizure of Jewish scripture from the community to which it rightfully belongs. Yet it is more likely that the 'Old Testament' will endure, oriented not towards careful observance of the details of the pentateuchal legislation but towards the ultimate divine self-disclosure in Jesus Christ — the external focal-point that offers criteria for assessing the varied literary material that is to be found within this collection.

The Pauline outline of a Christian 'Old Testament' invites further, more nuanced and careful elaboration. Indeed, it is characteristic of all the fundamental grammatical rules which this Pauline text helps to establish that they invite a theological elaboration that goes beyond the bounds of the canonical texts themselves. Thus, in Galatians, the single passing reference to Jesus Christ as God's Son (4.4) does not as yet provide an adequately worked-out basis for the assumption of his ultimate and universal significance; and since this is also true of other New Testament texts, a theological elaboration is required at this point which remains in conformity with these texts and yet goes beyond them. Similarly, there is in Galatians no attempt to relate the universal significance of Jesus Christ to the universal horizon of the creation (contrast Col 1.15-20), and this relative deficiency in the Pauline outline of an 'Old Testament' will have to be remedied — for example, in the theology that arises out of resistance to Marcion and the Gnostics. The theological relevance of a Pauline text derives in part from its invitation to participate in the theological reflection that it initiated and whose basic grammatical rules it helped to establish. The assumption that Pauline and other canonical texts are theologically sufficient and final risks transferring the ultimacy of Jesus Christ to a text which, however significant in establishing the foundations of Christian communal identity, does not in itself constitute an ultimate and absolute norm.

In this interpretation of certain aspects of Paul's letter to the Galatians, an attempt has been made to preserve the sharp focus of the literal-historical sense on the assumption that precisely this sharp focus might also be relevant theologically. This necessitated a criticism of the view that the significance of the biblical texts can emerge only when their historical particularities are dissolved into a generality comprehensive enough to encompass a readership whose situation is quite different from the one envisaged by the biblical author. It may well be that in many cases this anti-particularist hermeneutic is entirely appropriate. In the case of the Pauline text, however, it seemed worthwhile to try the experiment of dispensing with this hermeneutic, reading certain of the particularities of this text on the assumption that they remain foundational for Christian communal identity. If this theological appropriation of the literal-historical sense proves to be persuasive, then the relevance of Paul's text to 'our own concerns' is clear.

7. Creativity, Embodiment and Mutuality: Dorothy L. Sayers on Dante, Love and Freedom

Ann Loades

Dorothy L. Sayers was a fine literary artist, articulate about her own talent and how it flowered in her own writing. She was a Christian for whom incarnational and sacramental theology were of central importance. And whilst she had an unequivocal sense of each person's responsibility for her or himself, she unhesitatingly emphasized the mutual loving interdependence in which human beings best flourish. Creativity, embodiment and mutuality are marks of these themes in her life and work.

Through her discovery of Dante, she found her understanding of the experiences of love and freedom which had marred and made her own life transfigured in the writing of the great poet-theologian. Reading and teaching the *Divine Comedy* made her familiar with the vision of a Christian catholic in his engagement with the affairs of his day, capable of honouring and loving women, and of focusing all that he was and all that he believed in the adoration of the Trinity. This essay therefore begins with an introduction to Dorothy L. Sayers as a theologian writing on creativity and its freedom as a way of indicating why she would be fascinated by Dante, before turning to interconnections between freedom and love, embodiment and mutuality in his work as she interpreted it.

In the last fifteen years of her life, Sayers became something of an expert on Dante, notably as a result of translating and interpreting the *Divine Comedy* for Penguin Classics, and also lecturing on his work to specialist and non-specialist audiences. Although her Penguin Classics books are still in print, those lectures on Dante are not. Barbara Reynolds' book, *The Passionate Intellect: Dorothy L. Sayers' Encounter with Dante* is in part a justifiable plea for the republication of *Introductory Papers on Dante* and *Further Papers on Dante* which exhibit that 'passionate intellect'.[1] It is a phrase Sayers used of herself after she had used it of Dante.

---

[1] Barbara Reynolds, *The Passionate Intellect: Dorothy L. Sayers' Encounter with Dante* (Kent, Ohio: Kent State University Press, 1989).

A woman utterly bored with intellectual and emotional anaemia in doctrine, and above all if evident in supposed christology, she found in her reading of Dante a man 'sublime, intellectual, and, on occasion, grim', but also 'simple, homely, humorous, tender and bubbling over with ecstasy'.[2] Whatever he has to offer by way of a rigorous understanding of freedom can be appreciated only if we hold in focus the final ecstasy of Dante's vision of God:

> Power failed high fantasy here; yet, swift to move
> Even as a wheel moves smoothly, free from jars
> My will and my desire were turned by love,
> The love that moves the sun and the other stars.[3]

A recommendation to re-read Sayers on Dante is meant to function not merely to fill in an historical gap, so to speak, but to help to bring such neglected theological themes back into play. She, after all, found in Dante a theologian comparable to Aquinas, and capable of stimulating her theological appraisal of her own place and times. Lively appropriation of the past meant for her and could mean for us, an enlargement of vision and imagination, especially when theology is mediated by a great poet, rather than through the formalities of a certain kind of discourse possibly incapable of treating some of Dante's themes — such as, most notably, that of the vision of God and Dante's experience of his heart and will being turned by love.

The year 1993 was the centenary of her birth; and it is now half a century on from the first broadcasts of her twelve radio plays, begun in December 1941, published in 1943 as *The Man Born to be King*. These are by no means her only writing of what I suppose we have to call 'religious drama' whether performed in cathedrals or on radio. Apart from this category of writing, another major theological publication was her neglected *The Mind of the Maker* (1941), certainly important not merely for the development of a Christian aesthetic but for an understanding of the experience of freedom and love by a creative artist in respect of her work. Some of her characteristic arguments on this latter theme can also be found in her contribution to the conference held in Malvern in 1941. Not a 'professional theologian' in the sense of having an ecclesiastical or institutional base of some kind (still rare for women) she was primarily a 'professional writer', though she has a wry comment to make on this in the Preface to *The Mind of the*

---

[2]   Dante, *Divine Comedy* translated by Dorothy L. Sayers (London: Penguin Classics), *Hell* (1949), *Purgatory* (1955), *Paradise* (1962 completed by Barbara Reynolds). *Hell*, 10.

[3]   *Paradise*, 347.

Maker: 'If one must use this curious expression. The theory that what writes is not the self but some aspect of the self is popular these days. It assists pigeon-holing. It is, of course, heretical — a form of Sabellianism no doubt ...'.[4]

She was obviously aware as many theologians are not of the way in which her theology was an act of interpretation of herself, and of herself as a writer of detective fiction and poetry (to mention only two of the genres in which she worked), not to be appreciative of Dante's achievement — the tiger to her cat as she was to put it. Certainly reading his work, translating it (an act of interpretation in itself) and writing commentary seems to have acted in a re-creative way so far as her own theology is concerned. And Dante would pass all the tests she set for trinitarian and christological orthodoxy in a writer.

She tests writers by correlating classical heresies with their artistic parallels, and such correlation undoubtedly has its dangers. One of these is the threat of destroying precisely that disinterested integrity in an artist she wanted to defend, by fostering a preoccupation with 'orthodoxy' at the possible expense of simply writing a good poem or play or novel, or carving a statue or whatever. Another is to place beyond criticism those artists whose work *did* survive the criteria of 'orthodoxy'. Still, she is to be commended for wanting a 'sacramental' view of creative free-dom, the human somehow giving us clues to the divine, clear that the artist was subject to the judgement of God and must not misuse his materials. The core of her position can be identified in her claim that to let ourselves be spoonfed with the ready-made is to lose our grip on our only true life and our only true selves.[5] The point about the criteria of 'heresy' in respect of writing is that they give us some sort of clue as to how judgement may be brought to bear on the arrogance of the artist insofar as she mistakes the value of what she has achieved. Heresy helps to identify misuse and failure. And it is at least a novelty to think that even the work of a writer of detective fiction should be so assessed, let alone the others she mentions:

> There is, for instance, artistic Arianism — all technique and no vision, like the machine-made French-bedroom comedies and that slicker and more mechanical kind of detective story which is nothing but an arrangement of material clues. There are the propaganda novelists and dramatists — Manichees, whose son

4 Dorothy L. Sayers, *The Mind of The Maker* (London: Methuen, 1941), p.x.
5 Dorothy L. Sayers, *Unpopular Opinions* (London: Gollancz, 1946), p.18.

assumes what looks like a genuine human body, but is in fact a hollow simulacrum that cannot truly live, love or suffer, but only performs exemplary gestures symbolical of the Idea. There are the Patripassians, who involve the Father-Idea in the vicissitudes and torments of the creative Activity. Patripassian writers are those who (in the common phrase) 'make it up as they go along'; serial writers are strongly tempted to this heresy. We might, I think, also class as Patripassian those works in which the Idea insensibly undergoes a change in the course of writing, so that the cumulative effect of the whole thing when read is something other than the effect to which all its parts are supposed to be working.[6]

The Mind of the Maker was written when she had given up writing detective fiction and could reflect on her own achievements and what they meant to her, in line with those statements in the creeds of Christendom which purport to be statements of fact. She was not concerned at this juncture with those statements which were historical, but with those which were theological, that is, about the nature of God and the universe, drawn up 'under the urgent practical necessity of finding a formula to define experienced truth under pressure of misapprehension and criticism'.

The Christian affirmation is ... that the Trinitarian structure which can be shown to exist in the mind of man and in all his works is, in fact, the integral structure of the universe, and corresponds not by pictorial imagery but by a necessary uniformity of substance, with the nature of God, in Whom all that is exists.[7]

Of course she knows how to make the appropriate qualifications of this claim that for instance, God is bound by no conditions of any kind, whereas the human artist can create only within the framework of the universe and its conditions, and out of its material.[8] We need not attend to her trinitarian theology at this point, but only to her conviction that creative freedom is central to God-likeness, and is to be expressed not only in worship and the work of artists, but in politics and economics, reverence for the earth and for the material. The grim substructure of hell, the equivalent of a few days spent among the cellars and sewers of a city (sordidness, suffocation, rats, fetor and gloom) is only there 'for the sake of the city whose walls and spires stand up and take the morning'. The saints in paradise are deeply preoccupied with politics in church and state, and the 'city' is the 'place' where they experience the vision of God.[9]

6   Sayers, *Mind of the Maker*, pp.140-1.
7   Sayers, *Mind of the Maker*, p.x.
8   Sayers, *Unpopular Opinions*, p.37.
9   *Hell*, 11.

It is worth recalling a couple of points to illustrate how she became the sort of person who could come to the reading of Dante equipped with a thorough knowledge of a particular strand of the Latin Western Christian tradition (incorporating Athanasian orthodoxy) as exhibited in *The Mind of the Maker*. First, she was the child of a rural Church of England parish to which her father went from Christ Church, Oxford:

> I was born in a hollow
> At a confluence of rivers.
> I was brought up in a swamp
> Carved, caged, counter-checked like a chessboard
> By dyke and drain,
> Running from the Great Ouse to the Wash
> Where the wind never stops blowing;
> I know all about the smell that comes off the drowned land
> When the waters turn home in the spring
> (A peculiar smell — and I have encountered something like it
> In Venice,
> In the *piccoli canali* in the moonlight,
> Where it is considered highly romantic);
> I can say to the gadabouts:
> 'If you must have dank smells, you can get them in the fens of
> East Anglia ...'[10]

This may prompt recollection of Wimsey's experiences in Fenchurch St Paul in *Nine Tailors* of 1934, but we should attend not just to the flood but to his experience of 'being entranced by wonder and delight' at the sight of an East Anglian pre-Reformation angel-roof. Amongst many other things, Dante's *Comedy* is a text about angelic presence, angelic aid to human freedom, as in the case of the one who comes to make sure that Dante and Virgil can get into the City of Dis or Satan, one

> who walks the water of Styx with unwet feet.
> His left hand, moving, fanning away the gross
> Air from his face, nor elsewhere did he seem
> At all to find the way laborious[11]

Dante would make sense of a vision of hierarchy, order and otherness in inexhaustible variety, including that of 'super-human personality and differentiated power' as she was to call these

---

[10] From 'Lord, I thank thee' published in S. Jameson (ed.), *London Calling* (San Francisco: Harper, 1942).
[11] *Hell*, 125.

beings, a world which she inhabited without any sign of intellectual discomfort. She even put archangels 'on stage' in her 1937
play, *The Zeal of Thy House*, present to bring the cathedral
architect to admit his own pride. Together with *The Mind of the
Maker* this play is important in its attention to the way in which
the work of the creative artist stands in its integrity despite his
personal sinfulness.

Second, Sayers' clerical father taught her Latin from about the
age of seven, so that by the age of thirteen her French was almost
as good as her English and her German not far short. Here were
learned the elements of her skills as a translator, not only of the
Comedy but of such works as *The Song of Roland*, another Penguin
Classic. She translated this once on completing her course at
Somerville, and returned to it towards the end of her life. It was
published in 1957, the year of her sudden death. Its translation is
noteworthy for understanding why she did not complete the
Paradise volume of the *Comedy*. It is as though she drew breath
before tackling the translation of the last thirteen Cantos, themselves associated with such a profoundly moving story about their
discovery by Dante's son after his death.[12] Not only was the
translation incomplete, but also her introduction, commentaries
and notes to the whole, brilliantly completed by Barbara Reynolds,
but without the active reinterpretation of the text for her own time
so characteristic of the first two volumes of her work on the
Comedy. In particular, we cannot know what would have been her
final view of Canto 26, in which St John questions Dante about
love. The content of the last thirteen Cantos would give anyone
pause, but she was fascinated with Dante's world. Roland himself
was youth and gaiety personified, and she rightly says that his
death scene is curiously moving. In her own work, the warrior
penitent at the moment of death and trusting himself to God (not
just Roland, but characters in Dante's *Purgatory* too) had already
been presented in dramatic terms in *The Just Vengeance* (1946),
written for Lichfield Cathedral, straight out of her reading of
Dante as the play's title itself suggests.

Having turned to writing detective fiction to make a living, she
was to find herself with a son to support in a household other than
her own, but even so, she never capitulated to the view that the
value of her creative work was to be reduced to its market value.
Given the birth of her son in 1924, it is not at all surprising that
a woman placed as she was should find that writing Nativity plays,
poetry and songs associated with Mary the mother of Jesus should

---

[12] *Hell*, 52-4.

express her own tenderness for her child. One set of lines from the *Paradiso* she translated was the first twenty-one lines of Canto 33, the first part of Bernard's hymn to the Blessed Virgin Mary, later incorporated into Barbara Reynold's translation of the last thirteen Cantos. These lines Sayers had translated and issued privately as a Christmas card in 1949, having included the first four lines in *The Just Vengeance*. Just as she believed that *this* man was very God, so she believed in 'the personal operation of the Mother of God'[13] Mary being the supreme but not the only symbol of grace for Dante. Amongst those human persons who mediate grace to Dante,[14] there are especially in the *Comedy* Beatrice, his particular God-bearing image, and Lucy, illuminating grace, who together with Mary are 'a threefold image of Divine Grace in its various manifestations'. Here for Sayers was the recognition of an analogue of the Trinity for Dante — the basis, image and gift of which she had written in *The Mind of the Maker*: 'Mary, the absolute Theotokos, corresponding to the Basis; Beatrice, the derived God-bearer, to the Image; Lucy, the bond and messenger between them, to the Gift'.[15]

If we ask Dante what freedom is for, the answer must include setting someone free for loving. Sayers reminds us of the effect of Beatrice's *salute* (both 'salutation', and 'salvation' is meant) upon him, even the hope of it. He tells us that he would feel at such moments that he had not an enemy in the world.

> Indeed, I glowed with a flame of charity which moved me to forgive all who had ever injured me; and if at that moment someone had asked me a question about anything, my only reply would have been: 'Love', with a countenance clothed in humility.[16]

Meekness within and overflowing charity to others are signs of grace, and we can connect this with Sayers' comments on the stage in *Purgatory* where those suffering the penance for the root sin, pride, have prayed the 'Our Father' in Dante's paraphrase for this particular sin, directed to the virtue of humility.[17] In Canto 12, the Angel of Humility erases the sign of pride from his forehead, and she says we need to recall the contexts in which Dante uses the word 'humility' such as the one from the *Vita Nuova* just quoted, to understand the 'shimmering radiance of its angel', for 'The

---

13 *Purgatory*, 39.
14 *Hell*, 82.
15 *Hell*, 328.
16 Dante, *La Vita Nuova* translated by Barbara Reynolds (London: Penguin, 1969), p.41.
17 *Canto*, 11.

connotation is always of peace, sweetness, and a kind of suspension of the heart in a delightful tranquillity'.[18]

Freedom is thus associated with the possibility of a 'deathless and ecstatic present', with the delights of heaven and its 'riot of charity and hilarity', the final freedom explained in Solomon's words on the resurrection[19] and in turn Sayers' rewriting of that passage, as it were, at the conclusion of *The Just Vengeance*. Notwithstanding his insistence that the exercise of freedom is one's own responsibility at the end of the day (compare Piccarda in Canto 3 with Cunizza in Canto 9 of *Paradise*), it is inconceivable for Dante that 'only-one-selfism' is the soul's destiny in heaven. Rather, it is the soul's state in hell. The mutuality of prayer is expressed in the 'I in-thee as thou in-meëst thee' of Canto 9 and the joy of that mutuality in the 'Lo, here is one that shall increase our loves!' of Canto 5. *Paradise* 29 expresses the Creator's delight in creaturely mutual loving:

> Not to increase His good, which cannot be,
> But that His splendour, shining back, might say:
> *Behold, I am*, in His eternity,
> Beyond the measurement of night and day,
> Beyond all boundary, as He did please,
> New loves Eternal Love shed from His ray.[20]

A creature can rejoice in its own being, reflecting back to God the joy and graces bestowed upon it. Remaining true to itself, and devoted to God, God desires that love should flow from all our fellow-creatures. In her own response to Dante's lines in Canto 28 of *Paradise*, on being drawn by love's cords, and drawing others by them, Sayers wrote 'For Timothy, in the coinherence',[21] which happens to be about a much-loved cat, and what he gave to his human fellow creatures and received from them in his turn!

There are many points of interest in *The Mind of the Maker* about freedom and love, such as the ruthlessness of love[22] closely allied to the capacity not merely to spare neither itself nor its object, but to pass even beyond the desire of happiness[23] to a capacity for sacrifice. These and many other themes she met in Dante, but with the emphasis precisely on the making or unmaking of a *life*, 'the drama of the soul's choice'. And as she was suspected

[18] *Purgatory*, 164.
[19] *Paradise*, 179.
[20] *Paradise*, 309.
[21] Published in *The Listener* 89:2294 (15 March 1973), p.337.
[22] Sayers, *Mind of the Maker*, p.104.
[23] Sayers, *Mind of the Maker*, p.109.

of arrogance in her trinitarian self-understanding as a writer of plays, novels and poems in *The Mind of the Maker*, she would immediately understand the possible arrogance of the whole project of the *Comedy*. Here was a poet unsuited to the career of the practical politician, a man of 'an unaccommodating temper, a blistering tongue, and an indecent superfluity of brains'[24] taking his vocation as poet and prophet of this drama seriously, but fortunately always treating himself with what she calls 'a delicate and disarming ridicule'. Dante, above all, recalls us to a view of ourselves which will not allow an incapacity for that kind of seriousness:

> We must abandon any idea that we are the slaves of chance, or environment, or our subconscious: any vague notion that good and evil are merely relative terms, or that conduct and opinion do not really matter; any comfortable persuasion that, however shiftlessly we muddle through life, it will somehow or other all come right on the night. We must try to believe that man's will is free, that he can consciously exercise choice, and that his choice can be decisive to all eternity.[25]

Sayers attributes such seriousness to the Christ of the Gospels and his judgement on sin. To ignore his divinity, and stick to his teaching is still to have to come to terms with his authority on this matter. Dante elaborates what she believes Christ taught:

> If we are ever to make head or tail of the greatest of Christian poems, we must at least be ready to understand what is meant by damnation, and why every believing Christian recognises it as a terrible possibility for and within himself, and why it matters to our comprehension of God and Heaven and Man.[26]

Christians are to take their lives in this world seriously, both what they do, and what they are, for it matters not only to them but so much to God 'that it was for Him literally a matter of life and death'.[27] This is expressed in three identifying criteria of Christianity in her understanding:

> for the central Christian doctrine is precisely that of God incarnate in matter, its central act of worship the bodily receiving of God's substance in the sacrament of bread and wine, and

---

[24] *Hell*, 37.
[25] *Hell*, 11.
[26] Dorothy L. Sayers, *Introductory Papers on Dante* (London: Methuen, 1954), p.45.
[27] Sayers, *Introductory Papers*, p.100.

its unique eschatological expectation the Resurrection of the Flesh.[28]

Three corresponding marks of Hell are the denial and refusal of 'God incarnate in matter' — Christ as the 'Enemy Power'; the final refusal and thus incapacity for that central act of worship; and the ultimate horrors of 'enfleshment' so hideously represented in the Cantos of 'Hell'. She is acute in her attention to Dante's lines about the suicides of Canto 13, 'each body evermore/Borne on the thorn of its own self-slaughtering shade'. Sayers interprets Dante here as understanding suicide as especially an insult to the body, so that the withered trees on which the Harpies feed express 'his conviction of the intimate and unbreakable bond between spirit and flesh'.[29]

One needs to read the Cantos of *Purgatory* to focus on Dante's discourses about freedom and love, but in preparation for such a reading, it is worth attending to some features of Hell. The inscription over hell-gate is

> Justice moved my great maker; God eternal
> wrought me: the power, and the unsearchably
> high wisdom, and the primal love supernal.[30]

Seeing eternal reality as cruel, meaningless and hateful is a choice. The free assent of a creature must be assent to the reality that she is a created being, whose end is to mirror God's glory to the utmost of her created capacity as in *Paradise* 29. The risk is that the assent will be refused, or with a bad grace.

> ... taking the situation as the theology of creation gives it to us, we see that the mere existence of a 'self' that can in a real sense know itself as 'other than' God, offers the possibility for the self to imagine itself independent of God, and instead of wheeling its will and desire about him, to try and find its true end in itself and to revolve about that. This is the fall into illusion, which is Hell. The creature denies, or rebels against, its creaturely status, and at once plunges itself into a situation which is bound to be full of frustration and misery, because it is at variance with the facts.[31]

---

[28] Dorothy L. Sayers, *The Poetry of Search and the Poetry of Statement* (London: Gollancz, 1963), p.51.

[29] *Hell*, 154.

[30] *Hell*, 85.

[31] Sayers, *Introductory Papers*, p.62.

Some do not even choose, and one of the most unnerving moments in Dante's 'journey of self-knowledge into the possibilities of depravity' is the experience of the Vestibule to Hell populated by ditherers:

> Here are the people who never come to any decision. Do we despise them? or do we admire their wide-minded tolerance and their freedom from bigotry and dogmatism? They discuss everything, but come to no conclusion. They will commit themselves to no opinion, since there is so much to be said on the other side ... They never abandon themselves wholeheartedly to any pursuit lest they should be missing something: neither to God, lest they should lose the world, nor to the world, because there might, after all, be 'something in' religion. They shrink from responsibility, lest it should blind them; they condemn nothing, for fear of being thought narrow. They chose indecision, and here in Hell they have it; they run forever after a perpetually-shifting banner ...[32]

Dante is inviting himself and his readers to get beyond the Vestibule, and of course there is no substitute for reading not only Dante, but Sayers' own splendid summaries of his journey and the sins he faces and has to learn to repudiate as he learns a taste for Paradise and Heaven. The first sign of that repudiation comes in Canto 8 when the words 'Blessed is the womb that bare thee' are addressed to him. This process continues in Canto 31 where he acknowledges himself as stung with the nettles of remorse, hating what he had most doted on, and fulfilled in *Paradise* 31:

> Thou has led me, a slave, to liberty,
> By every path, and using every means
> Which to fulfil this task were granted thee.
> Keep turned towards me thy munificence
> So that my soul which thou hast remedied
> May please thee when it quits the bonds of sense.[33]

Beyond that there is the experience of 'grace abounding' the vision of 'our Image' in the spheres of the Trinity, the love which held bound 'Into one volume all the leaves whose flight/Is scattered through the universe around'.[34]

The appalling alternative is, as she paraphrased Boethius, 'the perfect and simultaneous possession of one's own will for ever'.[35] Her argument about the refusal of the free assent of the creature to its Creator is a familiar one, but an explanation of the

[32] Sayers, *Introductory Papers*, p.132.
[33] *Paradise*, 329.
[34] *Paradise*, 345.
[35] Sayers, *Introductory Papers*, p.67.

fall into illusion and the preference for one's own will remains as
baffling as ever, without the acknowledgement of some element of
a doctrine of predestination of which she must have been aware,
but cannot give weight to except insofar as the souls in Paradise
delight in their particular place in the scheme of things. Baffling
or not, she found in Dante the imagination and the poetic skill to
represent the final refusal of good and God, in Dante's circles of
perverse and petrified choice, narrowing down to Hell's frozen
centre. We have met those who refused choice at the top:

> below them, the people who incontinently lapsed into evil
> through failure to control their choice, blown on the winds or
> sodden in the march-water of their passions; then the deliberate
> hardening of the will to the choice of the wrong made in full
> knowledge — the will to violence, the will to deceit — circle
> below circle of fire and filth and disease, down to the ultimate
> treachery in which all feeling, all intellect, every conception, is
> frozen.[36]

At the bottom is the corruption of beauty itself, aping the glory of
the Trinity, a monstrous three-headed parody fixed in his inimi-
table self-will, champing traitors in his jaws: 'the six wings of his
immortal seraphhood beat savagely, powerless to lift him out of
the ice of his obduracy, and increasing that ice by the wind of their
beating', idiot and slobbering horror.[37]

Of Purgatory, Sayers cannot with the same robustness claim
that it was taught by Christ, but rests her case for it on the grounds
of practical charity, and 'our sense of the communion between the
blessed dead and ourselves'.[38] The first point at which this is
emphasized is in relation to souls in Dante's invention of the state
of Ante-Purgatory, the state of those saved by accepting judgement in the moment of death but who are not allowed to begin their
purgation. These are those who have what they earlier chose,
which was delay, and they experience now a purely retributive
justice — the suffering of being held back from the cleansing pains
they now so earnestly desire.

> Generally speaking, the souls in Ante-Purgatory must wait
> patiently upon the love and prayers of the living. Charity is the
> rule: the charity of others, one's own charity towards others —
> this breaks the ban and privileges the soul to enter upon its
> suffering.
> But once we are past the gate, there is a subtle difference.
> Prayers are indeed asked for, and their effect will, in fact, be the

---

[36] Sayers, *The Poetry of Search*, p.240.
[37] Sayers, *The Poetry of Search*, p.240.
[38] Sayers, *Introductory Papers*, p.75-6.

shortening of the period of purgation. But there is no more question of asking that God may remit the suffering — only that the souls may perform their penance better.[39]

For the purposes of discussion and understanding of this process with the souls undergoing it, one has to enter the state of Purgatory, since as she puts it, 'It is not while undergoing the foretaste of damnation that one can engage in abstract speculation; it is as much if one can endure and come through unscathed'.[40] Having squeezed out from Hell's suffocating bottleneck to look again on the stars, then the intellect begins to function again, and enjoy its capacity for music as well as for discourse. There is and can be no music in Hell, for it is a place of hideous, chaotic and incessant noise. Music begins in the beauty of Purgatory, with the first sight of the ship of souls singing of their redemption. From this point the songs mount

> Like to the lark which soars into the sky
> Singing at first, and then, with utter bliss
> Filled to the full, falls silent by and by.[41]

The beginning of this music, and the soul's experience of it, should not obscure the fact that the pains of Purgatory are like those of Hell, and little lighter in some cases. The difference is in the attitude of those who suffer these pains, who want their crippling illusions to be burned away, so that judgement and will may be free, and soul 'may endure unscathed the unveiled light of reality'.[42]

> But when some spirit, feeling purged and sound,
> Leaps up or moves to seek a loftier station,
> The whole mount quakes and the great shouts resound.
> The will itself attests its own purgation;
> Amazed, the soul that's free to change its inn
> Finds its mere will suffice for liberation;
> True, it wills always, but can nothing win
> So long as heavenly justice keeps desire
> Set forward the pain as once 'twas toward the sin ...[43]

The first discourse on free will comes in Canto 16, where one soul endures the smother of anger, a kind of test case for 'determinism'.

[39] Sayers, *Introductory Papers*, p.87.
[40] *Purgatory*, 11.
[41] *Paradise*, 234.
[42] *Purgatory*, 15.
[43] *Purgatory*, 236.

For if anger is simply the result of a rigid determinism, it is a matter neither for blame nor for praise. 'It is useless, on the one hand, to be angry with anyone for doing what he could not help doing; and on the other, the anger itself is merely a mechanical gesture, as much determined as the behaviour which appears to provoke it'.[44] Whatever the conditions in which a life is set, and Dante indulges no fantasy in which the will is independent of those conditions, 'Light's given you to know right from wrong at need', and a well-nourished free will may and must govern itself in relation to its loves. Dante believes that it is love which is the seed 'not only of each virtuous action/But also of each punishable deed'[45] for it is created apt for love. Right loves are to be distinguished from reprobate loves by a 'counsellor-power innate' which guards the 'threshold of assent'.

> Grant, then, all loves that wake in you to be
> Born of necessity, you still possess
> Within yourselves the power of mastery.[46]

Significantly, then, a kiss may be both the image of a sin — say, the indulgent dallying with temptation of Paolo and Francesca (Canto 5 of *Hell*) or the image of salvation, as in Canto 26 of *Purgatory*:

> I see each shade, on swiftness all intent,
> Kiss one from out the other troop, and go,
> Not pausing, with this brief salute content.[47]

The meaning of Beatrice's salutation for him was that he could see in other humans beings as grace-bearers for one another, or as in the case of Francesca and her lover, the source of one another's damnation rather than salvation.

Finally, not the least of Dante's attractions for Sayers was Dante's unmistakable affirmation of the importance of Beatrice to him, albeit somewhat Gemma-like![48] Given Sayers' essays 'Are women human?' and 'The human-not-quite-Human' of the war period, her own earlier experience of Somerville and of being allowed to graduate only in 1920, she was to find in Dante a man who could in his evaluation of women differ in important respects

44 *Purgatory*, 193.
45 Canto, 17, 199.
46 Canto, 18, 207.
47 *Purgatory*, 273.
48 *Purgatory*, 35.

from Aquinas. Of the biology reflected in Canto 25 of *Purgatory* (the theory that the female's part in generation was purely passive) Sayers need only note that popular psychology and popular moral standards still remained faithful to this scientific theory, meaning by this presumably what we might now call the gender construction of associating the female/feminine with receiving and the male/masculine with giving. She need only note it, and not discuss it, because it has nothing to do with Dante's understanding of the way in which Beatrice represented for him the integrity of the intellectual, emotional, bodily and sacramental. Barbara Reynolds' book prints an entertaining letter from 1944 in which we can recapture Sayers' pleasure in Dante's unambiguous affirmation of Beatrice:

> I had an alarming vision just now in my bath. I had *both* Dante and Milton as evacuees. After a long wet day, which they had whiled away by reading each other's works, they sat one on either side of the fire, Dante like a mournful eagle in captivity, and Milton like a bull in the arena, whose eyes were beginning to roll dangerously. I said nervously, 'Well, well, it's been wretched weather, hasn't it?' Whereat Milton, ignoring me, suddenly opened his mouth and told Dante exactly what he thought of young women who gave their boy-friends lectures in theology. When he had finished, Dante rose to his feet, slowly unfolding to his full height until, like a black pillar, his form obscured the light of the fire, and then he spoke — but, like the *grido* of the sphere of Jupiter, the sound was so terrible that the sense escaped me.[49]

In comparing Dante's Beatrice to Elizabeth Bennet, she commended not only the poet's central and abiding sanity, but also the accuracy of his feminine psychology.[50] So what he has to say about love is not for Sayers marred by the tradition of Courtly Love within which he works, though for our time this will do no more than what she calls the 'ecclesiastical view' of male superiority. She wants to bring into play lines from *Hell* as well as *Paradise* to correct both these traditions, in such a way as in her turn to be a creative interpreter of them as Dante had been in his day. In Canto 4 of *Hell* there is the line, 'They do me honour and therein do well', and in *Paradise* 28 the lines:

The dances which remain display to view
Princedoms, Archangels, and one circle more

---

[49] Reynolds, *The Passionate Intellect,* p.186.
[50] *Purgatory,* 33-4.

With Angels' jubilation is filled through.
And all these orders upwards gaze with awe,
As downwards each prevails upon the rest,
Whence all are drawn to God and to Him draw.[51]

Her point is that human beings need to acknowledge the ways in which freedom and love may both honour one another and generously exchange places with each other on the ladder of ascent, and that the images and means of salvation may be recognized, as Dante recognized them, in both women and men.[52]

---

[51] *Paradise*, 304.
[52] Dorothy L. Sayers, *Further Papers on Dante* (London: Methuen, 1957), p.196.

8. God, Grace and Freedom

Colin E. Gunton

I. Varieties of Freedom

If one were to place on a spectrum the different theories of human freedom which have appeared in the history of thought, the two ends would be represented by, on the one hand, modern theories of the absolute void, and, on the other, highly deterministic views like that of Spinoza stating that freedom consists in the resigned recognition of complete determination. At one end, theories of the void see willed choice as absolute: an action is not free unless it is entirely within the undetermined choice of the agent. Insofar as it is determined by social context, education, tradition or anything other than the undetermined will of the agent, thus far it is not free. Such a conception of freedom necessarily serves chiefly as an ideal, although something like it appears in a number of modern writings, as scarcely needs pointing out. Indeed, it is clear that the modern idea of freedom as a void, an empty space in which an agent affects to operate with complete freedom of choice, derives from the rejection of God, as, for example, it takes shape in one of the fathers of void theory, Friedrich Nietzsche. Freedom is only truly freedom when the agent creates, *ex nihilo*, the form of action which is entered. To trace the conception a little further back, and to its motivating power, we can see in Hegel's theory of the unhappy consciousness the development of a view that to submit to the other, especially to the omnipotent other, is a denial of essential humanity. It is accordingly in the context of the modern rejection of God that freedom becomes the assertion of the self in face of that which would deprive of freedom. And because to reject God is in effect to reject any metaphysical context or matrix for human freedom, the void is ultimately all that remains.

At the other end of the spectrum, theories of more or less absolute determinism are also to be found, although in practice, I suspect, also mainly as ideals: for example, ideals of total scientific explanation which will in principle predict all future actions on the basis of the knowledge of present and past. Underlying such ideals in the modern age is the mechanistic theory of the universe, now apparently on its deathbed, but effectively still encouraging the scientism that would affect to explain every action as the necessary outcome

119

of the previous state of the universe. That, too, is a highly damaging theory, in depriving moral agents of that which seems to make them moral agents, their freedom to have done otherwise, and on which most notions of personality and responsibility depend. But it is characteristic of the kind of concept that fills the vacuum left by the loss of the concept of God in modern thought. Nature or evolution or the universe become the hypostatized agents from which everything derives, as by necessity. The pantheistic undertones of such theories scarcely require pointing out.

The two ends of the spectrum, absolute freedom and absolute determinism, are notable for the fact that they tend to turn into one another. The response to scientific determinism is often an advocacy of the ethics of the void — as in Jacques Monod[1] — while the vacuum left by the void is often filled by some form of political authoritarianism, as Edward Craig has observed.

> Quite apart from the instability of the world which it might easily encourage, it is psychologically unstable in itself. It is the philosophy of the confident man, or, as its opponents would very likely have it, the over-confident man. Should that confidence flag it offers no secure consolation. The image of the void, from being a symbol of the limitless liberty of the agent, becomes a menacing abyss waiting to engulf all his purposes and reduce him to a nullity.[2]

Accordingly, neither extreme, the one a denial of our rootedness in the material universe, the other a denial of our personal transcendence of it, can be finally satisfying, for reasons that will appear below.

Most theories of freedom would appear to lie somewhere between the two poles represented by absolute freedom and absolute determinism. In the writings of post-war analytic philosophy there are to be found debates about whether, and in what way, freedom and determinism might be supposed to be compatible. For the most part, such attempts are based on the assumption that what I have called poles or the ends of a spectrum are the fundamental possibilities, and have in some way to be reconciled. Their background, too, is, fairly clearly, to be found in a deterministic view of the world culled from mechanist theories of science. And they bring me to a first major point. The theories I have reviewed depend upon a particular view of the moral agent as subsisting in some form of unmediated

---

[1] Jacques Monod, *Chance and Necessity: An Essay in the Natural Philosophy of Modern Biology*, translated by Austryn Wainhouse (London: Collins, 1972).

[2] Edward Craig, *The Mind of God and the Works of Man* (Oxford: Clarendon Press, 1987), p.271.

relation to the universe, and it is that which in this paper I wish to contest. They share an implausible conception of the fully formed individual consciousness, will or reason either facing or being swallowed by the totally other universe — or some dialectic of the two. Such a dualistic picture is fundamentally unsatisfactory at whatever level it is considered because it ignores the webs of relation in which agents are necessarily involved. What will serve to make the whole debate different is the search for mediating factors which show the implausibility of what remains in many modern discussions the paradigm view of freedom.

Once we concede that freedom is not an absolute — an absolute qualification of, or absolute absence from, the individual human agent — we admit that there is of necessity a measure of mediation. Freedom, I wish to argue, is not an immediate but a mediated relation to other people and the world which is the realm and object of free human action. Our freedom does not come neat, but is in part mediated to us by our fellow human beings and by God. The place on the spectrum of any theory between the void and absolute determinism will therefore be determined by the weight and nature of the mediation: by the way in which we conceive our being particularly ourselves is dependent upon the mediation of the Other or others. Thus the spectrum of theories will contain a wide range of positions that take their distinctive character from the nature of the mediation that is involved. Unlike the extreme positions, they are not based on the supposition that it is a simple matter of deciding how far I can escape from it, how far I can in some way evade determination by the universe by asserting my independence. The quest is for freedom as a relational category. At the centre of the question of mediation is the personal dimension, although our relation to the material universe is not irrelevant. For the purposes of this paper, however, under consideration is the contention that what it is to be a free human being is bound up with our relations with other personal beings, and it is that especially which widens the range of possibilities beyond the extremes of determinism and the void. That is why even the supposedly most extreme versions of the Augustinian or Reformed positions — those of Augustine himself, Calvin and Jonathan Edwards, for example — are not absolute determinisms of the scientistic kind, because they involve the interposition of some form of personal agency. And that is where the question of grace enters the debate.

II. Mediated Freedom

Two main theses are to be argued in the remainder of the paper. First is that freedom, before it is conceived as free or undetermined choice or willing, should be conceived in terms of, as a function of, personal particularity. In such a reformulation of the question, all the traditional foreground characteristics of freedom remain important: self-determination, moral responsibility and the rest. But without some prior consideration of what kind of beings make choices and behave responsibly or irresponsibly, their meaning hangs in the air. So that, adapting or misusing Luther, I would propound the following pair of theses:

1. Freedom is that which I do with my own particularity, that which enables me to be and do what is truly and distinctively myself.

2. Freedom is that which others do to and with my particular being, in enabling me to be and do, or preventing me from being and doing, that which is particularly myself.

To make the first claim is to say that to be free is to realize what one distinctively and particularly is. To make the second is not to deny it, any more than Luther's second statement that the Christian is the servant of all is to deny his first that the Christian is the free lord of all. It is to expand the meaning of the first, and to say that one's self-realization, one's freedom, is something that depends integrally and not merely contingently upon one's relation to the other.

The claim can be illustrated quite simply. If you incarcerate me, either literally or metaphorically in, for example, an intolerably adversarial professional relation, then you thus far deprive me of being myself.[3] Freedom is a relational concept in the sense that it cannot be understood merely individualistically. If we are free, it is in large measure because others enable or empower us to be free. Freedom may be something that we exercise or fail to exercise as particular beings, but our particularity is at the same time something that comes to us from the other beings with whom we are related. That point needs to be stressed strongly because it flies in the face not only of the fashions of the age, which tend to see the person as the individual engaged on a quest for self-fulfilment, a conception interestingly questioned in recent times by Charles Taylor,[4] but also of the individualist assumptions of much of the Christian tradition's theologies of grace and justification, which sometimes appear to present the relation between the individual soul and God as the only significant one.

---

[3]   We might want to say that the latter is worse, because it is our relations with others that so determine what we are severally able to become, but that is not the matter with which I am concerned at this stage.

[4]   Charles Taylor, *Sources of the Self: The Making of the Modern Identity* (Cambridge: Cambridge University Press, 1989).

Before, however, that first thesis can be developed, the question of the relation of God and human freedom must be faced. And here it must be said — and this is the second major thesis — that whatever the failures of the tradition, it is right in its fundamental contention that the prior mediating factor for human freedom is the relation to God. The fact that we are creatures and not creators of ourselves, as void theories imply, means that our relation to God is determinative not only for who and what we are, but for how we conceive that freedom of which we are speaking. That is a point which is neglected in many of the discussions to which I have alluded, partly for the reason already mentioned, that modern theories often presuppose the necessity of rejecting God, or at least of supposing him to be minimally relevant to the question. But once the God-relationship is thrown into the ring, there is no question but that it will have a major bearing upon this question, as upon any other. The complexity of the topic of freedom arises therefore not from the dialectic of void and determinism but from the fact that because there are many competing, or at least diverse, accounts of the human relationship to God, there are also many ways of answering the questions of what human freedom is and of the respects in which it exists.

The human relation to God must be understood on two levels, the second of which will be the chief concern of this paper. The first level concerns the doctrine of sin. The claim of the mainstream Augustinian and Reformation teaching is that, in point of fact, the condition of the person apart from grace is not one of freedom, but of slavery, and, to boot, a largely self-imposed slavery. If we are to come to terms with the human condition, we cannot evade the almost self-evident truth of the doctrine of sin. The misuse of freedom renders the agent in certain major respects unfree, a slave to self and to necessity. In support of that thesis I can call such diverse figures as Paul, John, Augustine, Anselm, Luther, Calvin, Kant — in certain aspects of his moral theory — Coleridge, Barth and Niebuhr. That said, there are rival accounts of how the lost freedom is to be granted or restored. The inconsistencies of Kant's view, which is the chief rival today to the Augustinian-Reformed account, have been the subject of two recent studies, and it is worthwhile pausing to look at them because of the light they throw on both levels of the human relation to God.

Gordon Michalson's achievement in *Fallen Freedom* is to elucidate the contradiction at the heart of Kant's *Religion within the Limits of Reason Alone*. He shows that the disturbing element, both in that book and in relation to Kant's philosophy of autonomy in general, is the concept of radical evil. Here Kant comes very near to the traditional Christian doctrine of original sin, teaching that

'Radical evil is "innate" but "brought upon us" by our own free-dom.'[5] Again in correspondence with the Christian tradition, Kant has a doctrine of moral regeneration, but this clashes with what Michalson rightly takes to be 'close to being the animating center of Kant's entire philosophical anthropology', 'the idea that we "make ourselves"'.[6] How does Kant escape the corner into which he has painted himself? According to Michalson, by adopting a theory of dual perspective. By looking at things from the perspectives of both eternity and time, the divine and the human, Kant purports to achieve a theory of salvation by grace which is in no way contrary to his theory of autonomy. But, particularly in view of his Newtonian determinism, he cannot:

> Kant tries valiantly to translate [his] appeals to divine action into commentary on the psychology of the moral agent ... If he eliminates the vagueness and becomes more blunt in these appeals, Kant unduly compromises both the rationalism of his basic position and the integrity of his fundamentally mechanis-tic outlook. But without these appeals, he runs the even greater risk of leaving the moral agent in defeat and despair.[7]

Kant wants a theology of grace, but is prevented from achieving it for philosophical reasons. His relation to the Western Christian tradition's theology of grace is therefore a dialectical one. On the one hand, he rejects it in the name of autonomy, but is too clear-eyed about the human condition to reject it *in toto*. On the other, he is in continuity with that tradition in attempting to reconcile Platonic and Hebraic strands in moral philosophy. As we shall see, earlier attempts to develop a theology of grace similarly fail to achieve a satisfactory synthesis.

But before we conclude this section, it is worthwhile pausing to outline another recent study of Kant which casts a rather different light on his moral philosophy. *Grace and Law* is a study of Paul's moral philosophy by a Jewish specialist in the thought of Aristotle and Kant. Heinz Cassirer's fundamental contention is that, even leaving aside Paul's teaching on grace, his analysis of the human plight is more convincing than Kant's. Central to his argument is the contention of the insufficiency of the rationalism and dualism of reason and sense that Kant simply presupposes. '[I]f the correctness of this assumption be called in question — as it surely

---

5   Gordon E. Michalson, Jr., *Fallen Freedom: Kant on Radical Evil and Moral Regeneration* (Cambridge: Cambridge University Press, 1990), p.8.
6   Michalson, *Fallen Freedom*, p.38.
7   Michalson, *Fallen Freedom*, p.128.

must be — it is found ... that Kant has no other argument at his disposal to support his assertion that man's reasoning power is responsible for his consciousness of moral obligation.'[8] Cassirer proceeds to argue that in *Religion within the Limits of Reason Alone*, Kant modifies and strengthens his thesis, and thus sharpens the contention between himself and Paul, so that 'the point at issue between them is not the facts of the case but the manner in which they are dealt with.'[9] Here Paul is right, Kant wrong: 'only a love as overpowering and ever-abiding as the one he describes will ever be capable of remedying so deep seated a malady.'[10] The conclusion is inescapable. The failure of the Kantian account of salvation means either that the human condition is beyond help or that the Augustinian-Reformed position is right. Without grace taking shape in atonement, without, that is to say, the mediation of Christ, human freedom must be understood to be at best curtailed, at worst virtually ineffective. Paul's statement is therefore definitive: 'by the grace of God I am what I am' (1 Cor 15.10). But in coming to this conclusion and working out its implications, we must remain aware that for some good reasons, the modern mind finds it unacceptable. 'So long as one remains within the Kantian orbit, one is committed to the view that giving the principle of divine grace admittance into the moral life of man must have the effect of degrading man and depriving him of his dignity.'[11]

This consideration must be kept in mind as we come to the second and, for our purposes, the crucial level at which the human relation to God must be understood. Suppose that in some way or other, there does take place in Christ a restoration of that relationship to God without which there is no true human freedom. What is its form in the present? Does freedom have to be mediated continually, or is it, once given, an absolute and disposable possession, like some form of gnostic enlightenment? The traditional answer is that the continuing relationship too has something to do with grace, not the grace of atonement, but the grace by which some continuing form of authentic human action is made possible without depriving the agent of freedom. People like to speak in this connection of a dialectic, calling on that part of Paul's verse which was not cited above: 'I worked harder than any of them, though it was not I, but the grace of God which is with me.'

[8] Heinz Cassirer, *Grace and Law: St Paul, Kant and the Hebrew Prophets* (Grand Rapids: Eerdmans, 1988), p.64.
[9] Cassirer, *Grace and Law*, p.82.
[10] Cassirer, *Grace and Law*, p.28.
[11] Cassirer, *Grace and Law*, p.82.

Paul's actions are his own, but in a sense they are not. That is what D. M. Baillie famously called the paradox of grace, a paradox transmitted to the Western tradition by Augustine.[12] But what is this grace? Are we truly concerned with paradox and dialectic, or can some more systematically satisfying account be given of freedom in relation to grace? They are the questions that must concern us as we pursue the question of the mediation of freedom.

III. Grace

The notion of divine grace is best understood as a mode of God's action towards, or relatedness to, the creature and not as some kind of substance that God imparts to the creature. For that reason there is much to be said for P. T. Forsyth's objection to the expression in Newman's hymn, 'a higher gift than grace'. There can be no higher gift than grace if grace means a form of God's relatedness to us. If that is so, it would also seem right to say that the relationship of God to Adam and Eve in Genesis 2, before the Fall, is a gracious one, or with Rahner that all creaturely existence is in some way graced existence.[13] Grace is not something reserved for sinners, we might say, but the fundamental form of God's relation to the creature. But, as we have seen, the question of grace takes its most interesting shape in connection with the free human action that is supposedly mediated by it to those set free from a state of unfreedom. But is grace rightly described as 'it'? The problem with much traditional treatment, I can suggest without claiming originality, is that grace has so often been reified, turned into a thing, so that the mediator of divine action is effectively conceived of in impersonal, or, perhaps more accurately, only quasi-personal terms. Let us examine some of the problems before turning to examine the form of divine action in relation to the creature with which we are concerned.

The notion of grace as a way of understanding the mediation of divine action in such a way that human freedom is maintained is crucial to the Western tradition, and absolutely necessary if we are to avoid both the extreme concepts of freedom I have sketched and the various pelagianizing forms of theology that have arisen in their light. We can share with those who would distinguish between uncreated and created grace a concern to maintain the

---

[12] D. M. Baillie, *God Was in Christ: An Essay on Incarnation and Atonement* (London: Faber, 1961), p.114-15.

[13] To say that is not to accept the form that Rahner's theology of grace takes.

mediatedness of all divine action, at least in one sense of the word mediation. For the same reason we should also beware of all conceptions of direct divine action on the person or the soul, as in some of the ideas which Augustine explores and as in some forms of mysticism. The absolute dependence on God of any person or action may take away the very freedom which we are seeking to validate theologically, and indeed the heart of modern protest atheism and the quest for the void can be understood as a rebellion against forms of divine action which are not gracious.[14]

But what is meant by this distinction between mediated and immediate forms of divine action towards the world and the moral agent? It is not designed completely to avoid the notion of direct divine action, as if God is dualistically divided from the world and can act only through a hierarchy of being, of the kind presupposed in Aquinas' Five Ways, so that action at a lower level is always mediated by action at a higher, and ultimately by God.[15] On this kind of understanding, God operates directly on the soul, indirectly on lower forms of being, sometimes by means of secondary causes. It is not that essentially platonizing kind of mediation with which I am concerned. According to Irenaeus, divine action in and towards the world takes place through the action of the Father's two hands, the Son and the Spirit. According to such a conception, God acts mediately but directly. For christological reasons in particular we know that there is no need of a hierarchy of agency, because here we recognize the freedom of God to involve himself directly in the material world. This is important for our purposes for two reasons in particular. The first is because it suggests that the concept of grace as a kind of insubstantial substance took the shape that it did because of a dualistic and christologically deficient conception of the mediation of divine action. Thus many Western conceptions of grace appear to *replace* christologically conceived divine action in and towards the world. The second is that the concept of grace as a kind of mediating substance similarly displaces the notion of the action of God the Spirit, as Robert Jenson has argued in his treatise on the Spirit. The conceptual framework within which Pauline theology was developed in Augustine and Aquinas, he argues, caused the matter to be couched in terms of causal relations between substances — to be sure,

---

[14] That is the reason why apparently the same mode of response to God may be construed very differently by those with different theologies of grace. Thus the calls to obedience on the part of a Bonhoeffer and, say, an advocate of political authoritarianism will be construed very differently.

[15] Anthony Kenny, *The Five Ways* (London: Routledge, 1969), pp.41-5.

personal substances — so that what Paul called the fruits of the
Spirit came to be described as 'effects'. '(T)his ineluctably sets the
problem of the co-operation between the graceful God and the ...
graced creature. The problem has been the crux of all Western
theology.'[16]

If, in face of this, we rather concentrate on a verbal — or perhaps
adverbial — rather than substantial conception of grace; that is to
say, if we conceive grace as a function of divine action in relation
to the world, much is to be gained. In particular, grace will be
understood to characterize the mode of God's action in both Son
and Spirit. Thus, speaking christologically, we can say that the
grace of God *is* the action of God in Christ meeting sin and evil with
a particular form of action, namely that paradigmatically shown
in the death of Jesus on the cross, but also in all the ministry of
Jesus. That action has the content of a historic liberation from sin
by forgiveness and reconciliation, once and for all. But this
christologically mediated form of gracious action is not restricted
to past-historic instances, but also has a bearing on our topic of
continuing gracious and liberating divine action. The Letter to the
Hebrews, for example, is much concerned with the gracious action
of God the Father mediated in the present by the ascended Christ.
But, as we are chiefly concerned in this paper with the continuing
realization, by divine action, of free human action, it will profit us
to concentrate on the pneumatological dimensions of the matter,
for it is where the Spirit is that there is liberty. Therefore, the
definition of grace can be expanded. By the grace of God is meant
the gracious action towards the creature of God the Father,
mediated by the Spirit through the Son. Put otherwise, we can say
that by relating human beings to the Father through the Son, the
Spirit is the one who graciously liberates people and things to be
themselves. We must now explore how this notion of grace as the
liberating action of the Spirit can take shape anthropologically
and ecclesiologically.

IV. Grace, Freedom and Particularity

There has been in recent theology a measure of play with the
notion of Jesus as a model for human freedom, though this has
often been conceived moralistically, in a rather Pelagian manner,
rather than in terms of grace. One exception is, of course, Karl

---

[16]   Robert W. Jenson, 'The Holy Spirit', *Christian Dogmatics*, edited by C.
       E. Braaten and R. W. Jenson (Philadelphia: Fortress Press, 1984); vol.
       2, pp.126f.

Barth, though the suspicion must be that in his case there is a
tendency in the opposite direction, to conceive the relation of God
to the human Jesus in terms of the kind of unmediated relation
with which this paper is taking issue. His Christ demonstrates the
freedom of God more successfully than the freedom of man. We
therefore turn to Anselm of Canterbury for an approach to what
must on almost any account be the crucial question for a theology
of grace and freedom: what is the relation of the human Jesus to
the God who apparently required a form of obedience which
directed to his death a moral agent who manifested a measure of
reluctance? What kind of freedom do we see in the response of
Jesus to the requirement that he die on the cross? The answer for
Anselm is to be found in a characteristically Augustinian conception of freedom. His concern is to do justice both to the many
scriptural texts showing that the cross was willed by the Father,
and so a requirement of obedience by Jesus, and those that witness
his free acceptance of the burden.

In his treatment of the question, Anselm assumes what cannot
be assumed in the modern world, a rather authoritarian view of the
human relation to God, that 'God requires (the upholding of truth
and justice) from every rational creature, and that the latter owes
this to God as a matter of obedience.'[17] To interpret Anselm rather
freely, we might say that on this account the obedience of the cross
was the *particular* form that Jesus' free obedience took. It was, to
use the definition of freedom being used in this paper, that which he
did with his own particularity, that which enabled him to be and do
what was truly and distinctively himself. 'Christ himself freely
underwent death, not by yielding up his life as an act of obedience,
but on account of his obedience in maintaining justice, because he
so steadfastly persevered in it that he brought death on himself.'[18]
A distinction is therefore to be drawn between mere obedience, a
form of compulsion of the agent by God, and the obedience that takes
the form of faithfully carrying out that which is the agent's particular form of just behaviour. It leads Anselm to a statement of the
compatibility of obedience and freedom. 'For this is simple and true
obedience, when the rational nature, not of necessity, but willingly
keeps the will that it has received from God.'[19]

---

[17] Anselm, *Cur Deus Homo* I.ix translated by E. R. Fairweather, *Why God
became Man, A Scholastic Miscellany: Anselm to Ockham Library of
Christian Classics*, vol. X, (London: SCM Press, 1956), p.112. However
apparently unmodern this is, we should be aware of the fact that,
mutatis mutandis, it would be a view of the human condition shared by
a number of modern political theologies.
[18] Anselm, *Why God became Man*, p.113.
[19] Anselm, *Why God became Man*, p.116.

Anselm's treatment provides the parameters for a development of our topic, but, typically of the Western tradition, lacks an appreciation of the pneumatological dimension of the matter, perhaps because, as Jenson remarks of Augustine in this context, that tradition on the whole tends to treat the three persons of the Trinity as functionally indistinguishable.[20] But if we are to extricate ourselves from a causal understanding of grace as a quasi-substance bringing about certain effects, the functional distinction of the persons is precisely what is required. If Jesus is able freely to do that which is his particular calling, is not the mediator of that calling best understood to be the Holy Spirit, who mediates to him the Father's will, while — graciously — respecting his authentic humanity? 'Where the Spirit of the Lord is, there is freedom' (2 Cor 3.17). On this account, to say that moral agents are enabled by grace freely to do something is to say that they are enabled by the Spirit's action to do that which is the particular form of action appropriate to them in the present. (It must be acknowledged here that this grace sometimes takes the form, though not in the case of Jesus, if not of coercion, at least of unwilled and often unwanted divine pressure. Under the conditions of fallenness, that will perhaps necessarily be the case, as is illustrated by the call of Jeremiah and Jonah, the conversion of Paul and the events making possible the writing of Francis Thompson's 'The Hound of Heaven'. Does God coerce into freedom? In these cases, very nearly, it must appear.)

In the case of Jesus, then, freedom to be and do what is particularly his is mediated by the Spirit. But to remain there for our model of human freedom would be to forget the fact that our freedom takes shape in webs of human relationality. There is a horizontal as well as a vertical mediatedness to be taken into account. It was argued above, in the second of the adaptations of Luther, that freedom is that which others do to and with my particular being, in enabling or preventing me from being and doing that which is particularly myself. One's self-realization, one's freedom, is something that depends integrally and not merely contingently upon one's relation to the other. And that brings us to ecclesiology, by which is meant not merely the theology of the church in particular but also a general theology of human being in community; what Daniel Hardy has called created sociality.[21] But it is through biblical ecclesiology that we shall approach the matter.

[20] Jenson, 'The Holy Spirit', p.126.
[21] Daniel W. Hardy, 'Created and Redeemed Sociality', *On Being the Church: Essays on the Christian Community*, edited by C. E. Gunton and D. W. Hardy (Edinburgh: T&T Clark, 1989), pp.21-47.

In the earlier part of this section, something was made of the characteristic mode of action of the Spirit as mediating freedom to the moral agent, illustrated as that was by his relationship to Jesus. It is surely significant that in the New Testament, the Spirit is also characteristically presented as the mediator of life in community. If one way of understanding sin is as enslavement to alienating patterns of relations, freedom correspondingly consists in the constitution of, or liberation to, patterns of relationality in which one's true being is realized. As we have seen, the determinative false relation is the vertical one, with God, so that the corresponding freedom is the freedom to be and do that which we are given by Christ and in the Spirit to be and to do. This freedom is realized by atonement and forgiveness. But it is not a shapeless freedom, freedom into a vacuum, which is given. Just as sin takes shape, as the opening chapters of Genesis show, in a range of personal and social dislocations, so salvation takes shape in a matrix of new and reconciled patterns of relations. One of the functions of ecclesiology, accordingly, is to provide an account of how it is that the Spirit gives freedom not merely individually, as in the classical understanding of the forgiveness of sins, but socially or in community.

But where does *grace* come in here? The answer is that if we are intrinsically relational beings, the grace — gracious action — of God is to be understood as that whereby he realizes forms of relationality which can be described as free. By relating them to God in Christ, the Spirit at the same time and in the same act also relates the forgiven to one another. (That is why 'in Christ' there is no male or female, slave or free, etc.). The paradigm of this is to be found in the account of the sending of the Spirit in Acts 2, whose interpretation has long been obscured by a concentration on the signs and wonders in which the story is dressed. The centre of the story is not that, but the realization by the Spirit of community: community between the nations of earth symbolized by the reversal of Babel that is depicted, and community taking shape in the formation of the church which is stressed so strongly as the outcome of what happened. But how can this be understood to take shape concretely in the present?

A true community — any true community — is one whose patterns of relationality enable its members to be, as members, distinctively and particularly themselves. Far too much stress has been placed in the tradition on the unity of the church, which has for too much of its history both ecclesiastically and socially been the agent of homogeneity, at the expense of particularity and diversity. The interesting point here is that when the Pauline literature speaks of the Spirit in relation to the church, it is at least as much interested in diversity as in unity: or rather, *it sees the latter as constituted by the former.* Notice how the following verses incorporate in a few words most of the themes of this discussion, and particularly the twofold mediation with which it has been concerned: 'Now there are varieties of gifts, but the same Spirit; and there are varieties of service, but the same Lord; and there are varieties of working, but it is the same God who inspires them all in every one' (1 Cor 12.4-6). The point that should be stressed is that particularity is realized in community. But, and here we come to the link with the secondary features of freedom, it must be free community in the sense of being unconstrained and entered into voluntarily. It should not be suggested that freedom under grace, enabled by divine action, is not the exercise of the free human will. But it is a will whose direction is given shape by the patterns of relation in which it is set. It is not the freedom of empty space. Only in relation to God and to others can we be particularly who and what we are, and therefore only so can we be free.

Then there is a further point that has to be made. Freedom is, as I have claimed, something that is the expression of our particularity, albeit particularity in community. It is a gracious gift, of the God who forgives through his Son and relates us to others in saving ways by his Spirit. But because it is realized in community, we must understand it as a function of relationality also in that it is something that we receive from and give to one another. Grace is therefore something that marks liberating human action also, for it is a form of action in which others are enabled to be themselves. To schematize: whereas in the modern age we tend naturally to conceive of freedom as freedom from the other, this picture assists us in thinking of freedom as for and (deriving) from the other.

There are dangers of idealization in this picture. The way in which ecclesiastical life has taken shape historically has often submerged these aspects, though they are, I believe, authentically biblical. But although they have been submerged, they have not always been absent. What is to be hoped for in the light of all this is a change of priorities in ecclesiology, away from the two poles, individualistic and authoritarian, which are to some extent reflexes of one another, and towards an ecclesiology of the personal. And that brings us back to two of the major themes of the paper. The first is the relation between concepts of grace and concepts of the church. It was argued that previous doctrines of grace conceived as quasi-substantial tended to displace the personal, gracious, action of God the Father mediated by the Son and Spirit. There is a case for arguing that they have been contributors to the inadequate ecclesiologies, objective-institutional[22] and subjective-

---

[22] This is not to deny the values of institutionality, but lament the fact that it has taken forms which subvert rather than realize the personal.

individualist, which have so disfigured the Christian centuries. In the former, grace is something channelled by the institution; in the latter, a function of the individual's direct experience. The notion of grace as a form of mediated divine action which enables gracious human action, and particularly action in community, should enable some correction of the weakness, and serve to obviate the necessity of choosing between an institutional and an individualistic approach to Christian community.

The second is the question of the relation between uncreated and created grace, which led to some of the unnecessary complexities of mediaeval theology and helped to trigger the Reformation. The traditional form is stated by Aquinas: 'Grace may be understood in two ways: in one way as the divine aid that moves us to will and act well, in the other way as a divinely given dispositional quality.'[23] That is another form of the dualism that separates divine and human action rather than integrating them. According to the alternative being suggested here, uncreated grace is to be understood as the eternal gracious freedom of the love in which Father, Son and Spirit are from and for each other in eternity. God's being is eternally gracious because that is a way of characterizing the reciprocal love of persons. This grace takes temporal form in the gracious ways towards us of the triune God, in the economy of creation and redemption mediated by the Son and the Spirit. 'Created grace' is correspondingly not a substance poured into us or in some way bringing about effects in our action, nor is it only a form of divine aid, but consists in forms of gracious action that are realized in the free human response to the gracious Spirit. Thus two desiderata of a theology of divine action are achieved. The first is the relatedness of God and the world, by virtue of which the creation is able to become what it is called to be by virtue only of God's creating and reconciling action. The second is what can be called the *space* between God and the world whereby God, by his action, enables the world to be truly itself. Such a relation in otherness of God and the creature was not adequately guaranteed by the old theory, but is opened up by the personal form of mediation here suggested and so allows for a shaped freedom other than that of the void. Moreover, because it is truly gracious, divine action towards the creature does not deprive the agent of personal integrity, but constitutes it in its freedom, and thus in turn makes possible gracious forms of human action. For is it not a defining mark of grace that it gives due place to the other, and therefore enables the other to be free?

---

[23] Thomas Aquinas, *Summa Theologiae*, 1a 2ae, III, 2.

Index